W9-BIM-847

Biblical Women Unbound

Also by Norma Rosen

NOVELS

John and Anzia:
An American Romance

At the Center

Touching Evil

Joy to Levine!

SHORT STORIES

Green, a Novella and Eight Stories

ESSAYS

Accidents of Influence:
Writing as a Woman and a
Jew in America

Biblical Women Unbound

COUNTER-TALES

Norma Rosen

The Jewish Publication Society
Philadelphia and Jerusalem

Portions of this book originally appeared, in somewhat different form, in
Reading Ruth, Out of the Garden, and *Kerem.*

Manufactured in the United States of America

Library of Congress Cataloging-in-Publication Data
Rosen, Norma.
Biblical women unbound : counter-tales / by Norma Rosen.
p. cm.
ISBN 0-8276-0580-3
1. Women in the Bible. 2. Women in rabbinical literature.
3. Midrash—History and criticism. I. Title.
BS575.R67 1996
296.1′9—dc20 96-11502

Designed by Arlene Putterman
Typeset in Stone Serif by Innodata Publishing Services Division

With love, for

ROSE, ANNA, MYCHAL

Mother, Daughters, Sisters, Wives, Warriors

Contents

A Personal Note

I am a woman whose immediate family left religious concerns, beliefs, and affiliations behind. By good fortune, grandparents were part of my growing up, still speaking Yiddish, still, in my grandmother's case, observant. Called for by her daughters at the synagogue in Yom Kippur starlight, she climbed down from her long fast in the women's balcony, to be scolded for undermining her health.

Like many of my third-generation American contemporaries whose families, intent on Americanization, omitted Jewish education from their children's curriculum, I have been drawn, fascinated, back to biblical beginnings, studies, texts, and, though in a far less headlong way, finally back to practice, observance.

Fascinated but frustrated. The power of ancient biblical narratives is often marred for me by the peculiar voicelessness of the women, Matriarchs powerful enough to deflect the course of covenantal succession, yet almost never the enactors of narrative. Add to that the anonymous daughters, the passive wives, the handmaids given to husbands, the breeding contests among women, the females thrust through doors at rapists to save the lives of men—how can one not question?

In their dream of entering America and drawing me after

them, my parents gave up on the Bible and its anachronisms, the old Orthodox synagogues with their peculiar combining of exalted yet lowered locating of women. Yet I loved the grandeur of the Bible as my father—a poor boy whose family could not spare his earnings for education—all his life loved secular intellectual grandeur, speaking with reverence of judges, lawyers, and "brilliant professors"; as my mother loved, almost in secret, the idea of God.

I wanted to think about the lives of Sarah, Rachel, Rebekah, Esther, Deborah, and Miriam in a way something like Dante's visit to the Underworld, where he met and questioned the suffering dead. Mine would be to the Overworld, to these mothers of the race. Shielding my eyes against their glory, I would ask my questions. These mysterious lacunae in your lives, of act or response—how shall we read them? As elliptical as God's "I am that I am," the glory of the Matriarchs' answers: "We are what we are."

Where were the commenting texts that could speak to contemporary scruples?

My own need to bring these powerful figures from our past into contemporary perspective is partly what propelled me to write this book. In doing so I had to acknowledge problems, name questions that stand between me and the text. I decided I could do this best by writing new midrash about women of the Bible using techniques available to me as a novelist, techniques close to those used by the ancient midrashists themselves. (For the moment I'll define a midrash as "a story"—singular: midrash; plural: midrashim; midrash can also signify a type of writing, as in the English word "narrative.")

Along with sympathetic imagination, I have brought a great curiosity to midrash of the past. As a practicing fiction and essay writer and a long-time teacher of creative writing, I am struck by connections between the mind of the midrashist and the fiction writer. I will explore some of those connections in the Introduction.

Implicit in each new midrash is a dialogue with the ancient rabbinic midrash writers who allowed their imaginations to play upon these powerful but cryptic stories from our past. Patriarchal that past undoubtedly was, yet classic midrash often shows astonishing sympathetic imagination for women of the Bible—along with obtuseness, blindness, the prurience associated with salacious imaginings about The Other, and a failure even to acknowledge that a question might exist. Little wonder, since the midrashic writers addressed these matters more than 1,000 years ago. We are all bounded by time and culture, and future centuries will no doubt wonder at the obtuseness of our own responses.

Still, there are questions to be asked now about the behavior of the actors in these biblical dramas that have so powerfully influenced Western civilization, and that still occupy a central place of reference as metaphors of our own lives. Through extended narrative, through newly imagined context and action, my stories reflect contemporary interests, ironies, skepticisms, scruples. But they also strive to incorporate spiritual longings. It is no small thing, I know, to aspire to bring these figures closer to us without losing their original power, yet such is my impudent hope. Such is my goal: to examine the narratives in which these glorious women figure, and to examine as well the ancient midrashic insights that question and embellish their stories. To question the questioners, always men: "Why did you think of that question, not this question, when this one is for me the one burning for answer?" To add the questions that occur to us now, to engage the traditional midrashists in dialogue.

Once, when I was privileged to study for a few sessions with a great talmudic scholar, I took advantage of a unique moment to ask a question about the text, "Do not place a stumbling block before a blind man."

Adam and Eve in the Garden of Eden, newcomers to the world—weren't they like the blind, I asked? Why did God set stumbling blocks, forbidden trees, in their path?

That, replied the talmudic scholar, was a question the sages said should never be asked.

The truth is, nothing seemed as important to me as asking the question the sages said should never be asked. In this way, we sometimes suppress questions for whose difficult answers we yearn, and settle instead for those whose answers we know will more readily come forth.

I hated to hear myself or anyone else spoil with debate those hours of prepared rabbinic commentary. Yet I wanted to ask, "Why *not* ask that question?" How did the ancient sages, and how did that very modern sage, our Talmud teacher, find it possible to live without asking?

To these questions the answers cannot be, "Such things were never done." Scruples cannot be silenced with moonbeams. Midrash is not a fairy tale of happy ever after, but a delving into deeper reality that allows the thorns to remain

in place. Spirit and flesh are still torn. Not poultice, but naming torn places is what brings relief—or revives our resolution to live in the tension of no relief.

It was tempting to think of writing a midrash about every woman of the Bible. Every one of them needs a midrash, every one needs a supplement to the slender space allotted her Bible voice. The 14 to whom I have given their own stories must suffice here. Eve, Sarah, Rebekah, Rachel, Leah, Miriam, Tamar, the nameless daughter-wives of Lot whom I call Goneril and Cordelia, Deborah, Bitiah the daughter of Pharaoh, Esther, Ruth, and Naomi. Additionally, Hagar appears as a strong antagonist in the stories of Rebekah and Sarah, and Yael and Zipporah are given voices in the stories of Deborah and Miriam. Mothers, daughters, sisters, wives, warriors: These categories blend and overlap. And men, of course, appear, as they must in every story of women. Fathers, sons, brothers, husbands. But for this moment, no warriors.

An exception to the pattern of a separate story told in the voice of the biblical woman is "Dialogues on Devotion," where five contemporary women discuss relationships in *The Book of Ruth.*

The story of Ruth and Naomi has been beloved through the ages, subject of many poems and paintings. Yet even this beloved story of lives reborn from ruin, of happiness snatched from misery, of human goodness and mercy that bring about human renewal, can, when looked at with a contemporary eye, show itself vulnerable to gaps, schisms, holes in the fabric of narrative through which our willing suspension of disbelief can seep away. We may turn from the story indifferently. "Yes, yes," we say, "another tale of a good girl who did as she was told and in the end earned herself a life of security." In "Dialogues on Devotion" a group of contemporary women gather to discuss and argue about *The Book of Ruth*—argue with one another and with the text, trying to draw closer to it.

In a sense, this makes "Dialogues on Devotion" a paradigm for the volume. It expresses my belief that unless we first work through our contemporary skepticism and ironies, we cannot come upon Ruth, or any other woman in the Bible, in a new way, a way that suits us now.

I hope that this book will resonate for a readership looking for new ways to think about these ancient, timeless narratives, as well as for those who would like to enjoy the stories themselves.

Creation of new midrash is an attempt to carry the voices of the Matriarchs (I don't intend limitation to strict biblical definition; progenitors are everywhere) closer to our contemporary ears. New midrash can provide pathways of invention along which we and the women of the Bible may move nearer one another. And perhaps, in the end, nearer the intention of what we were always meant to know.

Jews made no idols to speak to God, no idols through which God was implored to speak. They made the Bible and its stories. In the stories God listened and sometimes spoke. Alas, that has ceased. But we can still say, *"Hineni."* Here I am. And here is another story.

Acknowledgments

I would like to acknowledge here at least some small measure of my gratitude to the following people:

Dr. Ellen Frankel, Editor-in-Chief at The Jewish Publication Society, who held fast to our vision of the book.

Dr. Anna Rosen, my daughter, who was my first reader, enthusiast, encourager, and canny critic. Jonathan Rosen, my son, who shared with me some of the contents of his allusion-filled mind. Rabbi Mychal Springer, my daughter-in-law, who encouraged and taught me. Dr. Robert S. Rosen, my husband, who began to teach me Torah long ago.

Rabbi Burton L. Visotzky, in whose "Genesis Seminar" at The Jewish Theological Seminary of America I conceived the germ of this book, and who generously offered suggestions while it was still in manuscript. Dr. Ray Scheindlin, who continues the "Genesis Seminar" into Exodus and beyond. Dr. David Roskies, an exuberant midrash encourager. Dr. David Kraemer, whose extraordinary Talmud classes I have been privileged to learn from over the years.

The Jewish Theological Seminary of America and its Chancellor, Ismar Schorsch, who have generously opened doors of learning to the belated; its brilliant teaching faculty, too numerous to name here, whose devotion to scholarship and openness to imagination are combined in a manner as wonderful as it is rare.

Francine Klagsbrun, who propped and encouraged, Ruth Slater, Dr. Wendy Goulston, who offered critical insights.

Other teachers and writers, including the astonishing outpouring of work by women scholars such as Aviva Zornberg, Ilana Pardes, Phyllis Trible, Mary Callaway, Elaine Pagels, Mieke Bal, Leila Leah Bronner, Tikva Frymer-Kensky, Susannah Heschel, Judith Plaskow, and many others.

The devoted ancient scholars who compiled midrashic commentaries on the Bible, as well as the prodigious modern compilers who produced two monuments to midrash: Louis Ginzberg's six-volume *The Legends of the Jews; Sefer Ha-Aggadah (The Book of Legends),* edited by Hayim Nahman Bialik and Yehoshua Hana Ravnitzky. In the beginning were their words.

The six women of Minyan M'at in New York who gave a dramatic reading of "Dialogues on Devotion" on Shavuot 1995 and helped me hear what was there: Jocheved Muffs, Beverly Schneider, Nancy Sinkoff, Mychal Springer, Nahma Sandrow, and Hannah Meyers.

My deep thanks to all.

Single Bible narratives sometimes range over a number of chapters and books of the Bible. In each case, therefore, I have selected one aspect of the narrative drama for illustration by Bible text.

Bible excerpts are taken from *Tanakh,* published by The Jewish Publication Society, 1985. Though the translation refers to God as "He," my midrashim do not.

Introduction

aggadah - stories } difficult
halakhah - law } distinction
sometimes

INTRODUCTION

MIDRASH AND THE BIBLE

The storytelling aspect of midrash—charming or exasperating, stolidly obtuse or wonderfully insightful—is what we are concerned with here.

In the vast compilation of Bible commentary known as midrash, much of it embedded in Talmud, only one genre, *aggadah,* is concerned with storytelling. Another, *halakhah,* addresses scripture with an eye to its legal aspects. It is usual to make this distinction between the two. The Bible was concerned with setting forth an ethical basis for the life of the ancient Hebrews, backed by the force of *halakhah,* Jewish law. Yet it is not always possible or desirable to make a hard distinction between the *halakhic* aspect of midrash and *aggadot,* stories. Both shaped our Jewish sense of ourselves. It is important to see what moral and cultural lessons were taught by Bible stories and their commentaries. Many of the commentaries, particularly those expressing attitudes toward women, became the basis of tradition, carrying legal force. How do those meanings strike us now?

Moral truths—as embodied in the Ten Commandments, for example—are eternal. But we have only to read the midrashic scholars to see (if we weren't convinced of it already) how great an effort every generation must make to give morality the necessary irresistible force of revelation, if it is to be a living source of ethical energy and not merely a curiosity of ancient times.

The midrashists—the word midrash comes from the Hebrew *lidrosh,* to search, to ask, to explain, to draw out, to enlarge upon—seized upon improbabilities, gaps. These spaces lying open in the text set the scholars to dreaming, to imagining answers to their own questions. Often, the ancient commentators invented whole new tales that not only explained but extended biblical narratives. Midrashic methods can be a marvel of modernity combined with ancient materials. I will have more to say more about them in later sections of the Introduction.

Midrash that specifically addresses the stories of the Bible—*aggadot*—does so in various ways. It may use analysis, logical deduction, proofs by comparison, or "proof texts," passages culled from other texts and interwoven with the passage under study. And often it adds more story to the story. These added-on stories were sometimes invented by scholars in the heat of discussion, sometimes gleaned from legends and embellished with more comment.

Eric Auerbach's *Mimesis* notes that the Hebrew Bible in its terseness expresses moral teaching above all, in contrast to Homer's storytelling mode in *The Odyssey,* where details abound and aesthetics predominates over ethics. The Bible offers a detail-less simplicity and almost unbearable tension. This is how Auerbach describes the *Akedah,* the binding of Isaac by his father Abraham: "Serving-men, ass, wood, and knife, and nothing else, without an epithet; they are there to serve the end which God has commanded."

For Rebekah, the well; for Isaac, the binding. She was generous and life-giving, he was nearly sacrificed. That is all the background the Bible accords this bride and groom, progenitors of biblical Jews, mother and father to our sacral selves.

It may be because Bible stories *are* as terse and as given to moral teaching as Auerbach describes that midrash was born. Some traditional midrashim that comment on Bible stories with these narratives, *aggadot,* elaborate on the stories with an interweaving of astonishing detail.

What is equally astonishing is that these midrashim do not always appear to express moral teaching. Or if they do, not in a way easily come upon. Sometimes detail reinforces the original intention of the Bible story. At other times it pulls the story in some other direction. The results can be seemingly absurd and gratuitous linkings, or marvels of insight.

The medieval Jewish poet Samuel ha-Nagid said, "Each one explained the verse according to his fancy and according to what came into his mind." All the same, says another source, "If you wish to get to know the One by whose word the world came into being—study the *aggadah.*"

To which I add the question, if you not only study the *aggadah* but write some midrash yourself—what then?

WHAT I WANT MIDRASH TO DO

What I want midrash to do is pick out the questions that have lain dormant and unnoticed in the story for 1,000 years, like rich archaeological treasure, or the bone of some paleontological missing link fossilizing under layers of shale.

I want midrash to give a voice to women in the Bible who have had nearly none. To be an advocate for biblical figures over whom the ages have kicked considerable dust, and to imagine their lives. To try to see, for example, what events might have changed Rebekah from a sheltered, passive girl to a determined, goal-oriented woman who could take covenantal succession upon herself. To raise new questions and add them to those the midrashists have already asked, and to attempt new answers.

How is it that Rebekah didn't know about the great drama of Isaac's life, the *Akedah,* Isaac's near-sacrifice by his father? It hardly answers to say that the story was intended to put an end to child sacrifice, and since Isaac was not killed that is all that need concern us. A narrative once set in motion is no longer entirely in the control of its author. It takes on its own life; its integrity demands that narrative lines be followed to the end. Narrative can act like the golem in the famous sixteenth-century legend, the giant manlike construction said to have been created by Rabbi Judah of Prague to protect the Jews. It was created for one purpose, but its own energies drove it to rampage wherever it could.

And so the text cries out for us to imagine what life was

like for Rebekah when she found out the secret of that day on Mount Moriah when Isaac was bound to the altar and Abraham stood above him with a knife. What happened after she made the discovery?

And what of the response of Isaac's mother, Sarah, to the *Akedah?* We are never in Sarah's presence again after that near-fatal episode. What if Sarah knew of Abraham's intention? What might Sarah have done?

As for Rachel and Leah, what was it really like for sisters to share a husband and compete for his sexual favors so they could bear sons? Could they ever resolve their rivalry? A wonderful midrash has come down to us from *Lamentations Rabba:* Rachel, to spare Leah humiliation on her wedding night, when Jacob thought he was sleeping not with Leah but with his beloved Rachel, hid under the bed. When Jacob spoke to Leah, Rachel answered in her own voice from under her bed.

As sometimes happens, the answer to one question raises another question that is even harder to answer. This beautiful and sensitive midrash is at the same time incredibly insensitive, because it never wonders what on earth it could have been like for Rachel to be under that bed, or Leah to be in it.

What questions can we ask about Lot's daughters, who procured their father's seed in the good cause of procreation, thinking they were the last beings left on earth, or about Tamar, who posed as a harlot to usurp her father-in-law's seed for a similarly desperate reason?

Or about Miriam, heroine of Exodus, who was honored

yet bypassed and punished beyond the bounds of anything imposed on other members of that family of prophets, who were so pleasing and at the same time so irritating to God?

We know a good deal about the private lives of Abraham, of Jacob, of Isaac, of Moses, of Joseph. But what do we know about the private life of Deborah, a woman of powerful public position, a general and a judge? What *could* her private life have been like in that era?

And what of Esther, whose story ends in political triumph, but who is left, at the end, still sacrificed to the swinishly swilling Ahasuerus. What happened when the trumpets of triumph fell silent?

Stories from the Hebrew Bible are the cultural heritage of Western civilization. Women of the Bible, particularly in their familial and societal relationships—Sarah, Rachel, Leah, Rebekah, Ruth, Esther, Tamar, Deborah, and others, named and unnamed—hold powerful places in our imaginations.

I would like to turn things about. What if those Bible women had knowledge of us? How would they tell us their stories?

This is a book made up of such tellings about a selected group of women of the Bible, often in their own imagined voices. Above all, I want to suggest possibilities for new points of view, to create a narrative climate that will draw readers to participate creatively in the asking of new questions and the imagining of new answers, new midrashim. These new narratives should be exciting and unexpected as well—good storytelling. In this way I am trying to bring biblical narratives in which women figure closer to our contemporary interests, ironies, and needs without, I hope, losing their original power.

Implicit in these new stories is a dialogue with the ancient commentators, the midrashists. The time- and place-bound parameters of their views of women are contrasted with contemporary concerns. The questions they asked—or failed to ask—about these powerful but cryptic narratives can be offset by the questions readers now want to ask and to have answered.

The Lost Voice of Women

In numbers of individuals, families, potential genetic inheritance, in stories, sermons, and studies, the rich-threaded fabric of lived lives lost in the lost Jews of the Holocaust, one-and-a-half million of them children, we read our bankruptcy amid new Jewish flowering. I believe we must, sadly, add to that loss the millennial prohibition against the voices of women in traditional Jewish culture and religious writing.

Where are the texts they might have left us, the variety of voices they might have lent to the sound of Jewish thought? Our ranks impoverished, we cannot ourselves go on thinning them by leaving out the female voice, by denying her turn to speak.

To give biblical women a voice is not merely to do a "feminist reparational" reading and writing. It is to attempt some fractional hint at those voices that might have been heard had our losses not been so great historically and culturally.

If we understand that we must as never before allow the voices of women to be heard now, in the present, we must also see the necessity of plunging into the past to release our ancient mothers from embedded silence, to retrieve them through imagination.

We Know More Midrash Than We Think

In Egypt, the enslaved male Hebrews had to work all night. Their wives came to them in secret in order to conceive. But then they were faced with Pharaoh's terrible edict of death to their infant sons. Therefore when the women gave birth, the children went into the earth where they flourished until they could burst out again in full-grown health.

Before I had any knowledge of this or any other midrash, I wrote in my novel, *Touching Evil,* originally published in 1969, a fantasy cherished by one of the characters in that book: All the Jewish children in Europe about to be destroyed by the Nazis were magically taken up into the wombs of their mothers again and kept here safe until deliverance.

The rabbis of the early centuries invented and perfected midrash, but if they hadn't, we'd have done it ourselves. The need, the wish, the dream of altering reality is as strong in us as is hunger or thirst.

Models of the Past

For inspiration we have many classic midrashic traditions. I want to cite two here, so strong they burn themselves into the text. One is the story of Abraham, Sarah, and Hagar. Midrash takes up the case of Hagar, the concubine who bore Abraham's first son Ishmael, and whom Sarah later banished with her son, causing readers to worry ever afterward about the compassion of the Matriarch and the ethics of the Bible. When Sarah dies, Abraham takes as wife a woman the Bible calls Keturah. Midrash picks up these open strands of the story, weaves them together, and tells us that Keturah turns out to be none other than Hagar! Thus midrash provides a new ending of unmistakable rightness, giving release to pent-up ethical and narrative tensions.

The other midrashic addition is found in the story of Esther, or rather of Vashti. She is summoned to the court by the King and refuses to appear. Therefore Vashti is banished, and room made for Esther to enter the story and become the favorite of Ahasuerus. From that position she derives the power to overcome Haman, the evil plotter against the Jews. A midrash in *Pirke de Rabbi Eliezer* adds that Vashti is commanded to appear naked. And that is wonderful but puzzling. Wonderful because it deepens the character of Vashti, whose sense of personal dignity is heroic, against the odds of such times. Puzzling because it diminishes by contrast the stature of Esther, who is in fact the one who ultimately, as the favorite of the harem, will be forced to appear naked before the king and his court. (No, the Bible text doesn't say so, but that does not preclude the inevitable from occurring.) Esther has no thought for personal dignity, and though she is supremely courageous and cunningly creative on behalf of the threatened Jews, her personal story is shadowed by the story of Vashti, who forthrightly refuses to collaborate in her own degradation.

The question remains: Why did the rabbis embellish Vashti's story in this way? Maybe they wanted only to emphasize the sordid excesses of the court. Whatever their reasons, as a result something happens to the subtext of the Esther narrative that remains one of the glories of detail- and story-enhancing midrash.

NARRATIVE METHOD IN CLASSICAL MIDRASH

In the Jewish religious world, time conflates, collapses. There is no before and no after. That miraculous simultaneity stems from the rabbinic idea that all of *Tanakh*—the entire Hebrew Bible: five Books of Moses, Prophets, and Writings—as well as later rabbinic commentary on it, was revealed at Sinai.

Interestingly, this ancient declaration of faith meets itself again in the latest scientific theories about time: If you venture out far enough into the realm of quantum physics, there also you encounter no limitation of time, no before and no after. There you find the simultaneity of the rabbis.

A superb example of this approach, this midrashic magic realism of time conflation, can be seen in the following legend. The second-century sage, Rabbi Akiva, refers reverentially back nearly ten centuries to the wisdom of Moses who would, says Akiva, have been able to explain the meaning of the crowned letters of the Torah. At the same moment, in order to learn the meaning of those crowned letters himself, Moses listens in at the Academy where Rabbi Akiva expounds the mystery of the crowns above the letters, ascribing their ancient secret knowledge to Moses!

On a less exalted level, but one of no less importance to the midrashic rabbis, was the troublesome matter of the long journey on which Eliezer the messenger escorted Rebekah from her home in Haran toward marriage to Isaac in Canaan. What about the sexual temptations, the rabbis wondered, of such prolonged proximity? What about protecting Rebekah's virginity? If you were heavenly ruler for a day, how would you take care of matters? Would you say that Rebekah's hymen became miraculously impenetrable? Or that Eliezer suffered from impotence for the duration of the journey? Or that a plague of sealed apertures descended on the travel party so that they were incapable of any movement except eating, evacuating, and riding their camels? The rabbis called on all these possibilities to explain other cases, but in this instance they contented themselves with saying that for safety's sake, God shortened the trip of many days to a mere few hours, and no nights at all.

This conflating of time gives wonderful license. I have availed myself of it to infuse women of the Bible with a contemporary knowledge and sensibility. We are present in their own time, and they are here in ours.

The Daring of Midrash

Our lives are limited to a single story. In fiction, too, as long as it follows a realistic line, lives are circumscribed by one destiny. But the rabbis had no trouble devising alternate events for Bible characters. And they did it long after the Bible was transcribed and the canon was closed. To get some sense of how momentous this is, I suggest we imagine some things about the western literature most familiar to us.

Imagine if, for example, after Charlotte Bront's *Jane Eyre* was published and canonized in all the Great Books courses, some brilliant, fearless writer decided to write a scene in which the madwoman in the attic, Mr. Rochester's cast-off wife, escapes fiery destruction in the house, regains sanity, and reappears at Rochester's door to claim her wifely due. (Or read Jean Rhys' variation in *Wide Sargasso Sea.*)

Or if, after Jane Austen's *Pride and Prejudice* had been published and canonized in all the Great Books courses, some brilliant, fearless writer decided to write a scene in which Mrs. Bennett, the addle-headed mother whose day and night thoughts are magnetized by the problem of how to marry off her daughters, steps forth to say she is sick of marriage matters, has been secretly studying Greek and Latin, and is now going off with the village spinster to open a bluestocking salon in London.

If you can imagine these things, you may still, as I do, have trouble entirely taking in the magnitude of the daring, in their own context, of the midrashic rabbis. It wasn't *Jane Eyre* or *Pride and Prejudice* they were adding to, after all, it was the Bible! It was scripture. Holy writ. And when they did it well, they did it in a way that stuck.

I have already mentioned the midrashic addition to Vashti's story. Yet every Purim when *The Book of Esther* is read, I have to remind myself that something I remember as Bible text is not. That is, I know that Vashti's nakedness is midrash, but it has so powerfully attached itself to the text that I don't think of it as extrinsic midrashic commentary, but as intrinsic text, ore of the original.

Another example of such daring is the brilliant midrashic conversion of Keturah to Hagar. Once you know this midrash of Hagar's return to Abraham's bosom you can never unknow it. It is burned into the story as simultaneous alternative reading. The same is true of the midrash about Rachel's compassionate crouch all night long beneath Leah's bridal bed on her unfortunate sister's wedding night.

These examples, in my view, show midrash at its most glorious, rivaling the revelatory power of Bible text itself. Exact, rigorous, explosively eloquent even in starkness, and eminently right.

These inventions come about neither through putting Bible text beyond imaginative bounds nor by riding roughshod over it. They come from intense experiencing of the text, wrestling with it, squeezing it to press out—express—its meaning.

There are other examples of alternative midrashic readings so startling and profound that they seem to have attached themselves permanently to the text.

One more example is the notion of Lilith, the rebellious alter-Eve, that accompanies the slender text of the creation story. Lilith is an astonishing imagining of the midrashic rabbis. In Lilith, the rabbis conjured up a female who was repugnant to every one of their stated claims for male-ascendant society. Yet this invented woman of theirs, this anti-Eve, this Lilith, with her powerful, open sexual demands, her flagrant flouting of every decorum otherwise imposed on women, so captured the libidos of the rabbis that she carries her rebellious energy through the ages to this day. More will be said of her in the introduction to the new midrash on Eve.

La Lecture infinie

The title of David Banon's *La Lecture infinie* (aux Editions du Seuil, Paris, 1987), refers to midrash. I translate it as "The reading that has no end" or "Infinite interpretation." Midrash, Banon writes, is "La tradition d'une lecture toujours recommencée"—the tradition of a reading that is always beginning again.

NARRATIVE METHOD AND THE USES OF STORY

Although some Bible stories may have been presented for nation-building reasons—the covenant of land (Abraham) and the redemption of the hopeless and despised (Sarah, becoming fecund in her barren old age)—the narrative nevertheless takes on a life of its own. Abraham and Sarah have become a real married couple, quarreling about other bedmates and clashing on how to bring up the children. They have come to represent qualities other than those intended.

One thinks of Shaker furniture, carved in austere utility for the most practical use, but in the process acquiring aesthetic dimensions. So these biblical characters, placed on a page to teach religious, national, and societal traditions governing everything from covenantal succession to female subservience, take on subtexts of astonishing depths. Into these depths the midrashist plunges, drawing forth fresh treasure.

In some narratives, I take my cue from the traditional midrashists themselves (as well as from contemporary fictional techniques) to make a collage rather than a single linear narrative. More than one view of character is possible. More than one time setting for a story. More than one way for the narrative to go, and it may go in all those ways simultaneously. More than one resolution may be found.

"What doesn't happen in reality happens in dreams; if not in this life, then in some other." In his transcendent story, "Gimpel the Fool," I. B. Singer puts these words into the mouth of Gimpel, a born midrashist if ever there was one.

Kabbalah describes the various aspects of God: Human events may be governed by one of God's aspects this time, another aspect another time. Consistency, which we deem a great good in bringing up our children, is not always available to God's children. This quotidian lack brings compensation; as a source of narrative surprise, no one could ask for more. "What can possibly happen next?" is as urgent a life question as a fictional one.

MIDRASH AND FICTION

For as long as there have been storytellers, there has been trouble with ending stories. Some tellers may be a little self-conscious about beginning, but that's as nothing compared with ending. No wonder the end of a story is daunting: It requires your own version of philosophy, psychology, cultural history, theology, and world view, all wrapped in one. The end of a story is a moment of truth, not only about the elements of the story, but about you, the storyteller—what you are and what you believe.

As a writer of fiction, I am struck by the way in which

the midrashic writing of the rabbis resembles the creation of fiction, with one important exception. Midrash, unlike writers' revisions, comes *after* the final story version, the one already in the Bible canon.

The rabbis took narrative already set, known, and codified, and felt free to make variations. If they didn't quite change the endings, they sometimes added episodes or details that so altered the overall tonality of a story that it is felt as a new entity, as in the story of Abraham and Hagar.

Much of what the rabbis did with midrash resembles the fiction-writing impulse. Midrashists ask themselves about motivation for what the characters do. What the text omits, they try to supply, sometimes imagining themselves into the feelings of a character. Accounting for discrepancies in the story, they make events plausible.

But midrash can also sometimes seem like alternative drafts of a Bible story. It still insists on its right to imagine what might have been, as if each character continued to possess countless possibilities beyond its Bible definition. Midrash can give voice to radically skeptical views; midrash can appear to deconstruct, though by its own lights it is *re*constructing.

To see just how remarkable and daring a method this is, let us look briefly at the pre-history of a famous nineteenth-century English novel, Thomas Hardy's *The Return of the Native.* In early drafts, Hardy depicts Eustacia Vye as a malevolent witch. When we think of that beautiful, mysterious, and darkly unhappy woman who appears in the published version of the novel, it's hard to believe that Hardy would have once so conceived of her. Eustacia Vye evolved in Hardy's imagination to one of the grand romantic heroines of English Literature. Having got it right in the end, having seen that her dark-souled silences were not the trappings of Satan but signs of one woman's tragic nature, Hardy does not slip back or smudge the page with his earlier conception. But suppose he had done that? He would have come close to the vertiginous effect of some midrashic tales.

The way not taken troubles us in our lives and in our imaginations. Choose a path and embark on it, in life as in fiction, and there's no going back. We live in linear time and can't recapture time past except in memory. Perhaps that is why fantasies—fairy tales, science fiction, magic realism—take such hold on our imaginations. They are a way to get around the melancholy facts: one life, one linear narrative time-and-space-span-life, and one death.

In writing fiction you can revise, erase, start again, but you don't as a rule depict two opposing courses of action for the same character at the same time. A novel like Philip Roth's *The Counterlife* can play with alternative lives, positioning itself within a contemporary genre of self-conscious and self-referring fiction. Classical midrash positions itself within the tradition of revelation, which is what makes its practice of inventing variations on biblical lives so startling—until, that is, we understand that revelation is seen by the midrashists to be ongoing, and to include what they themselves at that moment are saying. Having come to understand the process, we can still be astonished by the contents of the variations.

To take the case of Rebekah again, we have already seen what the rabbis conjectured about the long trip to Canaan that Rebekah, Isaac's bride-to-be, took in the company of Eliezer the servant. It was dangerous. Isaac's past made him suspicious, midrash shrewdly goes on (that near-slaughter by his father). He would wonder if the servant behaved improperly on the way. No doubt, the midrashists said, the journey was miraculously speeded up to a matter of mere hours for safety's sake.

Let us look a little closer at this example. Safety? *Whose* safety? Did the midrashists actually believe that Eliezer might have raped Rebekah? And this in perfect disregard of what the biblical text is so eager to have us know—that Eliezer is a faithful, steadfast, loyal servant who, at the sight of Rebekah, bows down and praises God! I count this one of the prime examples of how the ancient midrashists explained the verse "according to fancy."

But also, of course, with a certain disregard for the dignity and privacy of Rebekah who, according to one midrash cited in Louis Ginzberg's *The Legends of the Jews,* may already have been raped by her own father, pre-journey, as his "droit de seigneur," the authority of a king to sleep with a virgin before her marriage. And *Pirke de Rabbi Eliezer* records for us a midrashic conversation between Abraham and Isaac in which the father tells the son to check Rebekah manually to make sure she's a virgin, and then to show the result to Abraham before taking Rebekah as his wife. Yet so oblivious is the rabbinic midrashist of what strikes a modern reader as shocking violation that this information is included in the chapter dealing with "loving-kindness." Midrashically, Rebekah is treated less as revered biblical "Mother" and more as generic Woman, to be turned 'round and 'round on the spit of imagination, liberally basted with the sauce of the salacious.

Yet sometimes, as we have also seen, midrash can make connections of startling insight that deepen characters and the meanings of their relationships, through the use of that same unbridled and unintimidated imagination. The midrash on the Genesis story of Abraham taking Hagar as a wife after Sarah's death is the magnificent illustration here.

The Bible text occasionally capitulates to the power of two different versions of an event, as in the double creation story. In one version God creates Adam and Eve at the same time. In the other, God first creates Adam from the earth and then Eve from Adam's rib. The Redactor, who welded together the various Bible accounts, allowed both creation stories to stand, thus making new resonances. Some midrash is of such great power that it will, in the reader's mind, be taken together with Bible story, again making it resonate anew.

MIDRASH AND THEOLOGY

The midrashists lived in the dark era that followed the destruction of the Second Temple. We live in a time sick with Holocaust consciousness. *The Book of Lamentations,* read every year on Tisha B'Av, the ninth day of the Hebrew month of Av, is filled with scenes of suffering and despair. But the ancient commentators were able to say that the suffering caused by the Roman sack of Jerusalem was a result of Jewish sinning. A mind that could conceive of the Holocaust as punishment for Jewish sin would be a mind so filled with the ancient faith as to divorce it utterly from our own time.

In an earlier midrash on Jonah, included in my collected essays, *Accidents of Influence: Writing as a Woman and a Jew in America,* I addressed the question of the reluctant prophet. The traditional view of Jonah calls him a man obsessed with judgment who despises mercy. He won't go to the people of Nineveh to prophesy their doom because he knows God's mercy will ensure their forgiveness. Jonah, says the commentary, wants only judgment; God wants only mercy. In my midrash, Jonah in the belly of the fish encounters a kind of living theater. For three days, scenes of Holocaust destruction of the Jews pass before his eyes. By the end of three days, when the big fish ejects him, he's still no more inclined to go to Nineveh than before. Not, this time around, because he believes God will be too merciful, but rather because he cannot bear the idea of a God who is neither judgmental nor merciful but merely absent. To live a late–twentieth-century life is to live in a time of broken faith lines, of discontinuity. Midrash is a counterweighting commentary in the service of continuity, of faith in the primacy of Jewish text.

The alienation that women readers of the Bible have felt, coming upon large lacunae of fact and feeling, cannot be measured in the same scale as "the turning away of God's face" in the Holocaust. Yet at a certain distant point these two alienations intersect.

In "Dialogues on Devotion," which forms the last section of this book, a group of women who are discussing *The Book of Ruth* cry out rebelliously:

"Are we so willing to give up the beauty of our texts because we're women? On Shavuot, we celebrate the giving of the Torah!"

"To men, I'm tempted to say! Should we ignore the taking away of it from women?"

"But in revolt against that theft, must we empty ourselves of our own stories?"

"The truth is, men are as bereft as we are. Men or women—we live in the same sour, skeptical age. We've lost our absolutes."

"Maybe it's true that we all stood at Sinai, yet we nowadays stand in very different places, often without much relation to the Bible or to one another. Maybe through new stories we can struggle toward continuity."

In my own Rebekah midrash here, there are two different kinds of stories. The first one I consider to be in the tradition of apologetics for God. It bears a family relationship to the kind of midrash that explains why Sarah threw out Hagar and Ishmael: Ishmael was shooting arrows at passersby, even making sexual advances to Isaac. In short Ishmael was a bad influence—Sarah could not do otherwise.

And so this first Rebekah midrash addresses the question of how it is that no one ever told Rebekah that her husband-to-be was almost sacrificed by his father. On the journey back to Abraham's family, three attempts are made to tell

Rebekah. First, Eliezer tries to tell her, and the wind blows away his words. Then another servant has a try, and the camels bray and drown out his words in noise. The nurse and handmaids have heard the gossip on the way and try to pass it on to Rebekah but she herself silences them. Her brother warned her not to gossip with women on the journey, but to keep a modest demeanor, and prepare herself for her marriage. And so the messenger, the servant, and the handmaids come to a single conclusion. God *wants* Rebekah to be ignorant of the *Akedah*.

Certain of God's necessary acts, they acknowledge, are too terrible to be faced. And a young woman expected to bear new offspring to the race would be better off not knowing about her husband's near-sacrifice. If she knew, her zeal for increasing the population might be diminished.

The little introductory journey midrash accounts for the biblical story's oversight in leaving Rebekah ignorant of the great trauma of her husband's life. It thus also accounts for the possible cruelty toward Rebekah in keeping her ignorant until all was too late by stressing God's compassion and practical wisdom. The second part of my Rebekah midrash turns a very different way. But this first part is in the tradition of theodicy: Human pain that appears to come from God is explained as embodying another of God's purposes, which in the end will comfort and improve our condition.

In the same vein of midrashic theodicy-as-comfort (comfort to some) is the astonishing ancient midrash about Rebekah's treatment at the hands of her father. Though the elements of this midrash have already been described in this Introduction, it is worth recapitulating some of these elements here for the purpose of illustration.

Rebekah's father, Laban, as king of that land, took to himself the *droit de seigneur* and, in the quaint old phrase, "deflowered" his daughter just before she left on her way to become Isaac's bride. So the rabbis are concerned about the father's possible rape, as well as the messenger's, on that long journey. To what end would the midrashists want to say this? Did they harbor some erroneous idea about the conception of twins? Today we know that a single sperm fertilizes the egg from which twins develop. But did the ancient rabbis conjecture that if the father or the messenger had been the first, and Isaac the second, to impregnate Rebekah, the discrepancy between twins—Esau the bad seed, Jacob the good—would be accounted for?

At the same time Rebekah's cruelty to Esau, her own son, would be accounted for as well. Her cruelty in stealing the first-born's birthright from Esau would have been all to the good, wouldn't it, if he was in fact the offspring of an unworthy father!

But what about the matter of Rebekah's 20-year barrenness? Midrashic magic realism might have taken care of that, too. Perhaps through invention the midrashists might have hit upon what natural scientists have recently discovered: The female of certain vertebrate species sequesters the sperm of various mates in special internal pockets, in order to choose at leisure and with complete autonomy the one with which she will later impregnate her own egg. Whatever the reasoning of the midrashic rabbis, it didn't trouble them to cast the shadow of rape, incest, and miscegeny on Rebekah. A God-ordained bride is a God-ordained bride, and even shadows, the rabbis may have conjectured, come from God. We might also conclude that even a Matriarch is a descendent of Eve, and in the eyes of the Bible and tradition and certainly of the midrashists, already half-suspect.

Here is another ancient midrash, recounted in *Avot de Rabbi Nathan,* that bears directly on the subject of faith: A rabbinic scholar will not give up mourning for his son who died an untimely death. After the official mourning period is over, the rabbi still sits in darkness. People come to comfort him but he won't be comforted. He torments himself wondering what sin he committed to bring on this punishment. Finally a disciple says, "You have nothing to reproach yourself for. Your son fulfilled all the mitzvot of study. You can have a clear conscience." The man responds by saying, "You have spoken the words I needed to hear." From that day on he re-enters the world.

At this point the midrash that answers the question—How shall we be comforted after the death of a loved one?—raises new questions for me. To be comforted as the man in the midrash is comforted is to be living in a mental and emotional world far from the one I inhabit.

Yes, there are times we would do almost anything to hear that comfort. When life has gone to the edge of horror and beyond, we want to believe if we can that there is still meaning somewhere, that suffering isn't entirely random and unnecessary and unnoted. Moreover, the capacity to take comfort from the sense of a timeless presence beyond earthly suffering is one of the gifts encoded in the human spirit.

But to be offered comfort at the cost of creating an illusory world leached of the agony of human loss is comfort that cannot comfort. Unless we manage to take from it something close to what the mystics tell us about mindfulness: that it is the key to finding God.

To find in oneself the capacity to be mindful of the gift of creation, to feel grateful to God for the gift of life, is already to have found a way to God. The kaddish, recited by those who mourn a death, is a prayer of praise to God. Those who in their deep grief recite the words of prayer are already taking comfort, the comfort of being able to speak the words.

This seeming paradox might be better named "A Progress toward God." If we can create the comfort of God, God will comfort us. Evil manifestly exists. And God, goodness, virtue, and mercy exist. But these we must create anew, call into being, summon by being deeply, passionately mindful of them. And sometimes, alas, we can best summon this deep and passionate mindfulness at times of deepest grief.

Midrash, like prayer at its truest, is an activist response to existential despair. So, I would posit, the man who lost his son had a wife. She was not content to think that it was quite all right for her son to be snatched away because he had fulfilled the mitzvot of study. She had questions about why, and about what kind of relationship she could be expected to have with God, who responds in this way to a life of dedication.

She might turn out to be like Job's wife, who at the lowest point of despair said to her husband, "Curse God and die!" Or she might turn out to be closer to the midrashic version of Beruriah, the learned woman written of in Talmud who, when her sons died, broke the news to her husband with a parable: A man has generously loaned two precious jewels to another man. Should the lender not have the privilege now of recalling them to their place among his possessions? "Of course," answers her husband. And he is brought to submission to God's will before he knows that it is his sons who are the jewels.

Or this woman might write a midrash of her own. It would be set somewhere between rebellion and submission. There she would find some new way to express the human cry of loss, which is our ongoing task, both terrible and radiant.

Midrash, in the end, is theology, as well as questions, answers, details, reasons, fictions, truths—stories.

Mothers and Sisters

EVE

GENESIS 1:29–31

God said, "See I give you every seed-bearing plant that is upon all the earth, and every tree that has seed-bearing fruit; they shall be yours for food. And to all the animals on land, to all the birds of the sky, and to everything that creeps on earth, in which there is the breath of life, [I give] all the green plants for food." And it was so. And God saw all that He had made, and found it very good.

GENESIS 3:2–6

The woman replied to the serpent, "We may eat of the fruit of the other trees of the garden. It is only about fruit of the tree in the middle of the garden that God said, 'You shall not eat of it or touch it, lest you die.' " And the serpent said to the woman, "You are not going to die, but God knows that as soon as you eat of it your eyes will be opened and you will be like divine beings who know good and bad." When the woman saw that the tree was good for eating and a delight to the eyes, and that the tree was desirable as a source of wisdom, she took of its fruit and ate. She also gave some to her husband, and he ate.

COMMENTARY

Eve! The disobedience! The serpent! The apple! The sin! The corruption of Adam! The expulsion from the Garden of Eden!

Was ever any scandal more sermonized and written about? Was ever more hatred heaped on a woman's head than on poor Eve's? "Your fault, yours! You lost us that beautiful paradise! The garden where God walked and talked with us! The lovely wholeness and at-oneness that now forever elude us! And you gave us instead our neurotic fantasies, bad marriages, ungrateful children, and in the end sickness and death!"

This fanciful Bible tale, with roots in mythologies of countless other ancient peoples, would be to us now no more than a charming folk tale, naive expression of weary humanity's longing for the safety and certitude of nirvana, paradise, if it were not for the fact that we know it to be the matrix of centuries of persecution of women. Eve as Everywoman, source of the world's corruption.

Equally fanciful is a midrashic fantasy of Lilith, the female who balked at the very moment of her creation when she refused to accept Adam's idea of a proper mating position: Adam uppermost, Lilith below. "Why can't I be the one on top?" Lilith wanted to know. In punishment for the hubris of upward aspiration, Lilith was cast down into the role of demonic fallen one, ensnaring men with lascivious wiles, forever seeking human victims in her rebellion against God.

If we omit the demon aspect, there is a good deal of Lilith's mode of clear-eyed questioning in even the most submissive picture of Eve. "Why can't I eat a piece of fruit from a tree that looks as healthy as every other tree in the Garden where God said everything is good? Where's the logic of that?"

Eve fell and tore the world down with her. Such is the traditional Judeo-Christian view. Elaine Pagels, in her *Adam and Eve and the Serpent,* says that Augustine is responsible for putting the definitive brand of seductress and sinner on the female, through Eve. Eve is the birth canal through which evil is born. Sexual sin is very high on Augustine's list of accusations against Eve (it is very high on his list of accusations against himself in his *Confessions,* too). As we know from Louis Ginzberg's *Legends of the Jews,* the midrashic rabbis were there before him, claiming that the serpent had intercourse with Eve before Adam did, and working out an etymology for her name, Hava, meaning serpent. Eve was Adam's serpent.

In *Pirke de Rabbi Eliezer,* sexual jealousy is the key to Eve's disobedience. The angels are jealous of the new man and woman, as is Satan, and Eve is jealous of a possible other woman. Rabbi Eliezer makes of the forbidden tree in the Garden a kind of Bluebeard's Castle. Suppose, he says, a woman is given all her husband's wealth except "this house, which is full of scorpions." A man visits and says that in fact she'll find there not scorpions but jewels, which the husband intends for another woman. Therefore, says Rabbi Eliezer, Eve preempted the treasure before a rival Eve could get at it. As her jealousy was greater than her piety (naturally, since she was Eve), she fell into the trap from which she could be sprung only into a world of suffering.

In *Song of Songs Rabba,* Rabbi Yohanan takes a chilling though poetic view of the torment of women. He asks, "Why were the three Matriarchs barren for so long?" and answers that God wanted to hear from them. "O my dove," R. Yohanan tells us God said, "why did I make you barren? Because I desired to hear your thoughts. As it is written, your voice is sweet and your face is comely."

In the same vein we may ask, "Why did God place Eve in an impossible situation, with a forbidden tree smack in the middle of her Garden?"

The answer might then be this: God wanted to see what Eve would do when she was expelled. "O, my enchanting creature," God said, "why did I make you barren of obedience to my command in the Garden? Because I wished to witness your ingenuity. As it is written, you are the creator of a world of creators, born of your banishment."

What is Eve's side of the story? "All about Eve" suggests possibilities.

All about Eve: The Eternal Female through the Ages

Grieving Eve

First she had to find language for loss. God hadn't given that. "This is good," God said. "And this is good. And over there is forbidden."

That was all.

None of the animals died. Nothing disappeared. Nothing was lost. Adam came back to their nest in the grass every night. So how could she speak of it when it happened?

There were pleasant days and nights, and sweet smells, the friendliness of all the Garden's creatures, the late-afternoon visits from God, the sense of everything belonging with everything, nothing left out and no one lonely.

Suddenly, the whole world was gone.

In her travels, her exile, she picked up phrases. From Yiddish: *Vos geven iz geven, iz mer nishto.* "What was, was, and is no more." From French: *Où sont les neiges d'antan?* "Where are the snows of yesteryear?" From English, "Whither is fled the visionary gleam? Where is it now, the glory and the dream?" That sort of thing. But never anything that could express the loss of a whole world! Unhappy and hurt, she became:

Defensive Eve

For a long time Eve ran around the world, pleading her own case, like a defendant without a lawyer.

"What did I do?" she asked. "Was it so terrible? Really, what did I do? There was the tree. Everything was beautiful and good in the Garden. God said so, too. There was my own intelligence, and that was also good. The snake was someone I respected. Why should I set myself against the advice of a neighbor? Didn't Jethro advise Moses to set up judges, wise elders to advise him? Is arrogance a virtue? I alone had wisdom and the snake did not? This is how people learn! This is what it means to have community! We were helpful to one another!

"And really, what did my son Cain do?" asked Eve. "His offering was not accepted. *Therefore* he became bad.

"Cain didn't know how to kill his brother. Bang him with his pot? Bite him with his teeth? Hit him with a pruning hook? A ploughshare?

"You see how innocent we all were? Adam at first tried to mate with a goldfish. Abraham didn't know which part of himself to circumcise. Cain didn't know how to kill his brother.

"We were all innocent!"

Eve became one of those disgruntled people who write letters to newspapers, always trying to set the record straight. This is entirely unpaid work. She became a laughingstock among editors, who don't mind the free filler if it is overheated enough.

She sent copies to everyone she could think of, often to

gentlemen of the cloth, adding little notes in her hurried hand:

"Dear Rabbis, Reverends, and Electronic Ministers:

"You try to convince us that whatever happens is for the best. Suffering will deepen our characters and spread goodness. Or else it will bring the Messiah. Then we'll all be rid of this hard world.

"I lost the world I lived in once, and I can tell you that I'm not keen to have it happen again. Moving is hard on the nerves. I've spent a lot of time making this world homey. Put up the curtains of custom, you might say, arranged the furniture of fortune, tried to make the place livable with a plumbing upgrade and some squirts of polyurethane.

"Will you please give some consideration to those of us who had to make this kind of life change early on?"

"Yours truly,"

"Dear Job,

"Out here in a place that's no more Eden than where you are, I keep hearing about your life and hard times.

"At first I asked everybody, 'What did this guy do to get thumped?'

"You see how the culture brainwashes us! I *know* that you didn't have to *do* anything. But it's in the tradition, right? He must have brought it on himself. His kids die, his factory goes bust, he's up for Chapter Eleven.

"But you didn't do a thing! Always a good boy. Whereas

I, you will have heard, DISOBEYED! Now—this is what you should look at:

"First, God was seduced by the serpent, same as I was. The serpent said to God: You want knowledge? How your creatures react when things go wrong? Make this pact with me, take my advice, grab a bite out of this guy's life, this Job, then you'll know.

"Compared to that, what did I do? Bite a piece of fruit? It's laughable! Who did I hurt? Whose kids died? Who did I make break out in boils?

"Face facts. God the Omnipotent was beguiled by the serpent! I, on the other hand, didn't act *entirely* because I was persuaded. I thought, Let me use my head. God created everything here and called it good. Okay. Suppose God did say, "Don't touch that!" Then waited to see if I'd be smart enough, nervy enough, to touch and find out for myself. How did I know there weren't two Adams and Eves! Maybe God was waiting to see which Eve would show more pizzazz. Why should I be a loser?

"The rabbis decided the Torah is now on earth. It didn't matter to them if God intervened with miracles to support one point of view over another in a dispute. 'I don't care if the river runs upstream to prove your point!' they said, 'don't care if God speaks from heaven to say you're right! We decide here. It's for us to figure out.' And you know what witnesses at the time claim they heard? God's voice saying, 'My children have outsmarted me!' And chuckling.

"So where was the chuckling in the Garden in my time? Why wasn't the Torah in the Garden for me to figure out, which I was trying every minute to do! Adam was hopeless.

Never shook the clay from his feet or the dust from his brain or the gravel from his throat.

" 'Oh—do you think we should?' When I showed him where to bite so we could explore together. Fat chance!

"Since starting this correspondence, news has come that your fortunes are restored—congratulations! Another bunch of kids and everything! I understand that when things were bad your wife said, 'Curse God and die!' What's she saying now—'Oh, look, new children, even better than the others!'?

"God will certainly be wanting to hear from you—your gratitude and so on. Do me a favor and add this message from Eve. Say this:

" 'Now you've done it! You're not going to be able to fool anybody ever again that we are rewarded for being good and suffer only when we sin. Satan has your ear and always did. When I was good you punished me. And when I couldn't have cared less you made me fortunate again. Maybe you *meant* the world to be what you said it was. But then you got bored. Too many beautiful days. Too mechanical, all this cause and effect, like an equation. Good marks, bad marks, reward, punishment. All things set in their forms. A world that worked, for Heaven's sake! But no! You preferred to see what men and women would do when they were tempted, crushed, cursed, disheartened, cast out; see how ingenious they could be, how they'd start again, work from ground zero, pick up the pieces, lift their boot straps, use prayer instead of sacrifice, praise God in the depths of Hell, start new families when the old ones are blasted, knit up hope in the shadow of death, sing psalms on the way to the ovens.'

"So you see, Job? Hasn't God eaten the forbidden fruit? Hasn't God wanted to know what should not be known? All the ways that the flayed-alive creature crawls to comfort and will not say die? Knowledge of good and evil! Oh, how badly God must have wanted it, how bored with a creation that was all good! God bit and then we had to bite. We're made in the image of God's heavenly boredom with beautiful days. We crave the bite. But that's okay. I'm getting the voters to turn out here, and I hope you will, too.

"I appreciate your conveying my message.

"Best wishes and sympathy to you. Solidarity forever!

c.c.: Rabbi Harold Kushner, author of *When Bad Things Happen to Good People*"

Dreaming Eve

After a while Eve gave up defensiveness and accepted loss and pain. This opened the way to fantasy, to imagination for what was lost. To a dream of Eden again.

Eve dreamed that she encountered God on a city sidewalk. At first it was like meeting a former lover who had behaved badly. For a second she thought of passing without a nod. But the truth was she was too happy at the encounter to do anything so silly. (She didn't exactly see God; she had been walking along the street one minute, and the next she knew God was there—it was more like that.)

And then she had one of those dream conversations in which we speak without moving lips. She spoke inside God, and God spoke inside her.

—Why did we have to be expelled from our beautiful

Garden? My husband broke down completely after that. My children ran wild. They committed horrible crimes. And I am tormented! Desired, then despised as a bringer of death! Why did you make me suffer when you knew I loved you so?

—I? I expel you? I make you suffer? How could I do that, beloved? In the Garden I called and called. I looked for you everywhere, to bless your journey.

Eve discovered loss, from which came pain, from which came a time of relying on *nothing* but language, from which came fantasy and imagination for what was lost, from which came a dream of Eden again. This dream, this understanding of what was missing, wanted, needed, enabled her to shape a place for each of the children who came to her now, a place where, for a while, everything was protected and loving and kind. After that she was able to let them go, reminding them that they could always come back to the Garden she kept for them in her heart. She let them go without the brandished fiery sword, and without the disgrace, or the curses with which she believed herself to have been driven away (though she was surprised to learn that her children sometimes saw departure from their home-Eden as terror-filled, like her own).

She saw her experience differently now. Bitterness fell away. Her memories altered, softened, as children's do when they age and remember home.

After her encounter with the grieving, searching God, she saw with what reluctance she, the beloved, had been released from the Garden to freedom. Though it had been anticipated. The time of the flight of the child is always near at hand.

SARAH

GENESIS 18:11–14

And Sarah laughed to herself, saying, "Now that I am withered, am I to have enjoyment—with my husband so old?" Then the Lord said to Abraham, "Why did Sarah laugh, saying, 'Shall I in truth bear a child, old as I am?' Is anything too wondrous for the Lord? I will return to you at the time next year, and Sarah shall have a son."

GENESIS 21:9–13

Sarah saw the son whom Hagar the Egyptian had borne to Abraham playing. She said to Abraham, "Cast out that slave-woman and her son, for the son of that slave shall not share in the inheritance with my son Isaac." The matter distressed Abraham greatly, for it concerned a son of his. But God said to Abraham, "Do not be distressed over the boy or your slave; whatever Sarah tells you, do as she says, for it is through Isaac that offspring shall be continued for you. As for the son of the slave-woman, I will make a nation of him, too, for he is your seed."

GENESIS 22:1–3

Some time afterward, God put Abraham to the test. He said to him, "Abraham," and he answered, "Here I am." And He said, "Take your son, your favored one, 'Isaac, whom you love, and go to the land of Moriah and offer him there as a burnt offering on one of the heights that I will point out to you."

COMMENTARY

In Sarah's narrative, as in others, some traditional midrash seems *imprinted* on the Bible story: That Sarah taught Torah in her tent as Abraham did in his. That Sarah saw Ishmael in sexually indecent behavior with Isaac and therefore wanted Ishmael banished. That she died just after the *Akedah,* and her cries when she heard of it are the sounds of grief the shofar makes on Yom Kippur, the one high-pitched cry that goes on and on, and the broken stuttering cries.

Pirke de Rabbi Eliezer tells us that the serpent who betrayed Eve in the Garden of Eden was the one who told Sarah that Abraham had sacrificed Isaac. She "cried aloud three times and gave three howlings" and died.

With so much richness already in place, why does Sarah need new midrash? For one thing, the rabbis don't ask the question that seems obvious to us: How could Sarah, who taught Torah alongside Abraham, who heard God's voice clearly the first time when God announced the birth of Isaac, not know of God's ordering Abraham to sacrifice Isaac? Knowing, how could she not act?

Sarah was 90 years old when she conceived a child. She laughed at the divine announcement and wasn't the only one who had trouble believing it could happen. People said that Isaac was Hagar's son, too. That it was Hagar who had borne this second son by Abraham, as she had Ishmael, the first one.

As if to refute this tale, another came into being to tell us that Sarah had so much milk she was able to nurse 100 babies when she gave birth. Compared to the miracle of conception at the age of 90, such abundance of milk may be a minor manifestation. Inappropriate, though, and inconvenient. God doesn't know limits; we have to. "Did you think I wanted *that?*" we can imagine Sarah protesting.

There is much that is inappropriate in Sarah's story. Abraham felt forced to say she was his sister so that he would not be killed when Pharaoh took Sarah into his harem (Genesis 20:2). And this, midrash tells us, was because she possessed such physical beauty that her radiance shone through whatever coverings Abraham used to conceal her when they passed through the desert.

Hagar, Pharaoh's daughter by a concubine (*Genesis Rabba*), was the handmaid given to Sarah by Pharaoh. Sarah then gave Hagar as concubine to Abraham, who conceived Ishmael. Midrash adds that Abraham loved Ishmael's "playing and dancing," and Sarah was jealous for Isaac's sake. Was her Isaac perhaps not a lively fellow? A little clumsy, a little slow, not agile enough to elude Abraham when he bound him to the altar? Maybe the ram gave more trouble than Isaac did!

Sarah swore she was Abraham's sister to save her husband's life. What wouldn't she have done to save her son's? Her relationship to God was as intimate as Abraham's. Though not mentioned specifically, Sarah must have been present at the setting forth of the covenants, since God's instructions about the covenant of circumcision were clearly passed down through women: witness Zipporah's ability to circumcise Moses' son (Exodus 4:25).

So zealous a mother, so careful a hearer and watcher of God—how can we not wonder why Sarah wasn't an active intervener in the *Akedah?* For those of us who wonder, "The Unbinding of Sarah" follows.

The Unbinding of Sarah

It is not generally talked about, but on that dark journey up to Mount Moriah where Abraham was to sacrifice his son to God, Sarah also went along.

Naturally, she would go.

In the night she heard the voice in Abraham's tent saying, "Take your son and sacrifice him." It was a voice she recognized. That voice and Sarah had laughed together!

Sarah rushed into Abraham's tent, but Abraham waved her away. No talk! No time to listen! Preparations to make!

He had been more attentive when he sent Hagar from the house with Ishmael. He had been more reluctant to expel *them.* He had caressed *that* mother, kissed *that* child.

Now he pointed his finger away from himself and without another word or gesture expelled Sarah from his tent.

But Sarah stayed to argue. Naturally, she would do that. Maybe Abraham didn't know, maybe he hadn't understood? No one disputed that Abraham was a good man, but it didn't do at times like these to be too quick to obey! And since Abraham could think of a hundred questions to put to God about the sinners of Sodom and Gomorrah, surely he might have thought of one or two about their son?

"If you had no questions," Sarah cried, "why didn't you just laugh out loud?"

The busy Patriarch moved about the tent. His ears, having filled with God's voice, could take in nothing else. Preparing, preparing! He knew when to take God seriously. When to question, when to be silent.

And when to lie! Who knew that better than the two of them? Years ago it had been. "Save my life!" he'd begged. "Let me tell Pharaoh you are my sister, not wife. We will ask God's intervention, and you may be untouched. But even if Pharaoh should take you, it is my life, my life!"

She had not refused him. Abraham had led her as his sister into Pharaoh's palace, past the barbarous guards with flashing swords. Each antechamber was darker than the one before. In the darkening light of the torches' smoky gleam, she passed first through a chamber hung in gold and the green of the sea; next, through one of gold and the blue of heaven; the last was a chamber of gold and the red of blood.

In each room she trembled. In the room of green and gold she whispered, "Are you with me, Abraham?" And her husband answered, "Here I am." In the room of blue and gold she asked, "Are you here, Abraham?" "Yes, I am here." And in the room of red and gold she cried out, "Where are you, Abraham?" But there was no answer. Eunuchs had already seized her, pulled her through the door, and left Abraham outside. Within she was bathed, oiled, perfumed, and brought naked, with bells on her ankles and fine gauze scarves floating about her face, to Pharaoh. Later, God's plague descended and Pharaoh's women could not bear. But that was later. Always that little time lag before catching God's attention. Her husband had once more agreed to something to save his life and was telling the lie this time to her! Who could be sure when matters would come to God's attention?

During the night Sarah dreams of Hagar. There is no limit to the questions Sarah asks then.

—When death stalked your son in the desert, didn't you utter some prayer, some special supplication, that brought God's mercy down? You, whose son survived, can't you teach me words that give such blessing?

Hagar, no longer handmaid, is decked in full Egyptian robes and tasselling. She stares outward sybil-like, enthroned. In the perversity of dreams, she is now possessed of Sarah's former youth and beauty.

—I offer you aid, former mistress, Hagar answers. Not as measure of my love, but of my power. Your plight's more severe than mine. You, a mortal woman, wished my son's death. God himself desires the death of yours. Here's advice, voice of experience—submit! If you're worthy, reap reward and rescue. Otherwise, your son's as good as dead.

—Is that all?

—Yes, all.

—No words? No prayer? You, the inventor of prayer?

Sarah turns to go, then turns again. She falls to her knees. Weeps. Begs for Isaac's life.

—You must remember? Act or prayer? Hagar, something else you must have done!

The shocking dream scene! Sarah's embrace of her former handmaid's knees. Hagar's repulsion, with movements of feet, of her former mistresses' arms!

—I am about to impart the secret knowledge! Hagar intones.

But then the dream dissolves.

Sarah seeks Eliezer, faithful servant, Abraham's messenger. Him, too, she plies with questions Abraham will not allow.

"How can it be the life of Isaac God wants? He is the son God *gave* me! Why give a son, then take away? Is there some other truth we ought to guess at? What does God expect this frightful message will make us understand? If we understand, will we fathom to benigner meaning? Speak, messenger!"

Eliezer answers with care. "Messages are often longer than we think. Some go on so long whole wells run dry."

"Didn't I laugh when God promised a child? I laughed at the knowledge that I would not be allowed to keep him. I laughed, foreseeing bitter birth pains. My laugh was a vow to not love this borrowed boy, soon to be returned. Yet I was as helpless as if I'd never vowed, ready to sacrifice a bondwoman's son to save my own. See how life reflects our deeds! If I had not sent Hagar's son to banishment, might God now choose him for sacrifice and spare mine? Is that God's message? Speak, messenger!"

Eliezer replies, "I have already dreamed a journey Abraham sends me on. There is water in it. Water often means life. I remember feasting at the end."

"Did you feast as Abraham's inheritor? Once, Eliezer, you were near inheritor of Abraham, who had no son. Then two were born. One son vanished. Is the second to follow? Will Eliezer inherit at last? Speak! Speak!"

"If so, it would be misery to Eliezer. He is no Abraham, and has no wish to hear direct from God. Let his master pass God's word along in tasks, in praise for work well done. Let Eliezer inherit a night's sleep, and let the sons of Abraham live and strengthen, endure ordeals, if they must, from God!"

"Yet were you, in your dream, the inheritor of Abraham's house? Messenger, you must speak!"

"I was myself, a servant. Trusted on great errands. When I woke, my heart filled with joy. I had done my task, traveled far and yet remained in my true place as one into whose ear Abraham, who has the ear of God, pours messages."

Still Sarah will not let Eliezer go.

"Is there some other sacrifice God would accept? For this only son of mine—10 first-born bullocks? 20 finest kids of the herd? 30 sheep? 40 heifers? 50 fledgling birds? Or *your* son, Eliezer? Speak, messenger!"

But Eliezer is struck dumb.

In the morning, Sarah also took provisions, mounted a donkey, and rode to Mount Moriah. Naturally, she would do that.

No more questions. Her son had been 90 years coming, 40 years growing. Her only son, Isaac, whom she loved. She followed them.

Now and then Abraham looked back and saw her. He shouted something and the wind blew it over his shoulder. He made pushing-away movements with his arm. Sarah kept on. Naturally, she would.

Whenever she lost sight of them she called out to wayfarers, "Have you seen my beloved? I beg you to tell me which way he's gone!"

After a while she saw that Abraham and Isaac had dismounted their donkeys and were already climbing the stony mountain on foot.

"I am coming, beloved," she shouted to her son, so that he would understand nothing could harm him. But as she urged her donkey forward, the beast stumbled and stopped. She felt its trembling in her thighs. Something was in the path.

She saw nothing. No snake or scorpion. But she continued to feel between her thighs the shudders of the little donkey. Sarah and the donkey both trembled before the empty air of nothing on the path.

Then there were warm puffs of air on her cheek. The nothing on the path was drawing closer.

"Where are you, Sarah?" came a voice at her ear.

"Here I am, God, hurrying toward my husband and my only son, with whom you blessed my old age. Up there"—Sarah pointed urgently—"they're coming to the top!"

"Stop a bit. It's a long while since we've talked together. In fact, not since the day you heard prophecy that you would bear that same son. I'm afraid, Sarah, that you failed to take it seriously. You laughed."

"Did I? Such things escape my memory these days. Since you say so, of course I humbly apologize for it. But the truth, if you remember, is that I was already 90 years old. Past a woman's time for that."

"Have I shown myself partial to the young? On the contrary! In long, barren periods I age my chosen women. Then

I come to them with creation. What is time to me, Sarah, woman's or man's?"

"True, but I must hurry. I am in a terrible rush to get to my son in time. . . ."

"You harp on time. If it reassures you, I will stop time while we talk."

"Please don't, or I will have to do this all over again."

"Then I will *slow* time. For the sake of your righteousness and also your former beauty which I still behold perfected in my timeless eye. Come, be young! I count on you for relief. Lightness, a bit of lightness! My powers, tremendous, override all. My forces, my faces, my phases, they race and rage. Male toward female, mercy toward judgment, compassion toward law, wisdom toward—I forget exactly what. In short, Sarah, having imparted my effulgence, my aspects crash about, make runs to distant corners of my radiance like children darting to a base in hope of hearing a voice cry out, 'Allee, allee, home free!' The bark is chipping off the Tree of Life from constant glancing blows of my powerful, several, separate selves which you and your kind in creative covenant were to integrate with goodly acts. How well you've done this is attested to by endless tears and supplications on your side, and utter unpredictableness on mine."

"These are heavy matters, and I am . . ."

"Can't I make you see how it is? One phase pushes to the fore and smites with misfortune some good man walking in a field! To test, of all things, steadfastness! Another issues frightful orders to test viciousness among the virtuous! These matters vex me. I'd show more benign guidance to my human flock, yet suspect those free wills that I've given them run counter to my own! Sarah, much is darkening, I rely on you for lightness!"

Still mentally harping in her narrow, limited, human fashion on how time slipped away, Sarah could see all the same that this would be the worst of all times to forfeit her usefulness to God—terrible timing! She forced herself to alter tone and manner. Though her time-filled heart was thumping out its seconds full of fear for Isaac, she dismounted her donkey and leaned in simulated ease against a rock.

"What is your pleasure, O, my Maker?"

Puffs of warm wind touched all parts of her body. She felt a voluptuousness take hold of her flesh—was God turning her into a young woman again, was time really nothing? Though the rock she leaned against was hard, she felt exceedingly comfortable.

"To begin with, a chat. Tiferet—Beauty—and Bimah—Intelligence—must have risen. You needn't look impatient. How well fastened to your core are your own modes? Some years or days ago when I announced that you would bear a son—let's have no discussion about this now—you laughed. Yet, if I am not mistaken, you grew to love your son, Isaac."

"With all my heart."

"Yet your son Ishmael you also loved, did you not?"

"Of course I loved Ishmael! Did I not myself send Hagar, my servant, in to Abraham to conceive? I can still see the tent with its dark flares, its animal hangings, its low wide bed. Hagar, that Egyptian, danced toward the Patriarch, lured him there . . ."

Sarah's voice grew fainter, as if she spoke to herself,

"Hagar and I held hands across the old man's back. Abraham revived in the presence of youth. Why not I? Hagar's son became my own! His strength and sleekness became my joy! Then when I no longer prayed or hoped or wished for it, God's voice told me I would bear a child. God's joke, I thought, to embarrass an old woman. Saying, 'You will bear when I say to you: "Bear!" ' And did I not bear Ishmael on my knees?"

"Ishmael was the son of your knees and your bosom, Sarah, and very nearly of your loins. Yet you sent him out of your house with his mother to what might have been his death, for all you knew. Oh, I covered for you—I sent an angel with water before any real harm could be done. I promised Hagar that Ishmael would become the father of a nation of his own, and I kept my promise. But you, Sarah! How did you bring yourself to banish the first darling son of your heart?"

"Here I am," said Sarah, hotly defending herself, "an old woman now, and was old even then! An old person's love is cruel. Sees essentials, contracts to essence. Saves what must be saved. In my heart and body I was already a grandmother when I became a mother! Couldn't you *see* that?"

"Calm yourself, poor old mother—or grandmother, as you choose to call yourself. Did I not cause all the springs to freshen and flow once more? Did I not make you young? And can I not do it again, this very moment, should I so desire?"

"It's embarrassing," Sarah said, hiding her eyes. "If one's body is not one's own. Against my will I bore Isaac. But when he leapt from my belly to my arms, I leapt like a lioness to protect him. Danger was everywhere. In Ishmael, my darling boy no longer. I said to Abraham, 'Banish them!' I stanched his tears with my will and in place of Ishmael thrust my flesh!"

A puff of air sighed at Sarah's ear. "Beneath all that beauty, so much cruelty! Well, you are my creation, made in my image. More accurately than the male of your species, with his unreliable appendage! Had I *that* to do again I would build a male regenerative organ as dependable as the female's. Perhaps a retractable arrangement—you've seen the necks on my turtles?"

Sarah thought, While God rambles over Creation, what is happening to my son? Let me frame a shrewder answer and end this. "Yes, of course I know turtles. I also knew you would have plans for the slave-girl's child. Hagar was far too comfortable where she was. A slave's a slave, in the end. We gave her all the freedom there was, yet the slave within was too great. She'd lost ambition, and would have stayed in her position forever. A push through the door was what she needed. To enter her real destiny, I mean. Like your demanding that Abraham set out into the world when you told him to go. Suppose he'd been too lazy, or too satisfied where he was? He'd be nothing now. So Hagar and Ishmael went out into the world and their names grew great. And I, too, must . . ."

"An ingenious answer in its way. Yet tell me, Sarah." The puffs of wind on her cheek grew hotter. "Did you never long for your first child? Did you not miss his daring outspokenness, his surprising, flashy exploits? Is it only Isaac's meekness that speaks to your mother's heart?"

Sarah yearned to get away, up to the mountaintop, where her beloved must certainly be seeking her! Yet she could not hold back questions of her own.

"And when you formed us from the clay, could you not have shaped us misfortune-free? Where is the womb's free will? Does it choose to disobey you when it cannot send forth fruit? You, O God, can impregnate a stone, but I was created a woman who could not conceive. Can you not give up curiosity about your own creatures, to see what we will do when we face the worst of times? No water, no child, no land, no rest, no harvest, no friend, only enemies and slaughter—what will they do now? Can you not cease these tests, these researches in wretchedness?"

In the heat of speaking, Sarah at first sat upright, then rose to her feet. "Can you not bear to grant all your children the chance to prosper in this brief life," she said, moving purposefully in the direction of her donkey, "as any mother would?"

Sarah was stopped by the sound of what she thought was laughter.

"That *is* amusing. Women do not want that! They connive, and scheme, and choose one child over another, whom they cruelly deprive! I have seen it, and will see it again!"

At that, Sarah burst out: "It's *you* who make us choose! This child over that child! Time's cut too short, you have snatched away immortal life from us. We are forced to covet inheritance, how can it be shared? Humiliated by death, how can we not be cruel? You are bountiful, but there is never enough to go around."

Ominous silence. Sarah trembled. I have failed to amuse. I have lost, both time and Isaac!

"Take care, Sarah!" the voice rumbled in her ear. "I see that like Abraham you like to argue with your God. But I am not always in the mood."

"Forgive me if I spoke hastily. Although you have slowed time for me, my heart still runs up the mountain for my son's sake."

"Have I not managed to divert your purpose yet? Perhaps you'll reveal what provisions you have in your sack. Did you mean to find a shady tree and refresh yourself?"

"Your will be done," said Sarah. She pulled from her sack a male sheep that bleated in the light. "But let it truly be your will, and not some misreading by my husband's tired mind."

"What is your purpose here, Sarah? Surely you did not expect to slaughter and roast a sacrifice for me?"

At first Sarah was silent in protest against such teasing. But silence used up precious minutes. She answered, "This is why I must hurry to the mountaintop! To make sure my husband hears your command as you intend. Here is the sacrifice he must make to you. Not our son Isaac!"

"Are you so certain of my will, Sarah?"

"You who rescued a slave-girl's son will surely not demand the life of mine!"

An ominous pause, then the relief of God's words:

"Sarah, you have wit! The randiest of my creatures will butt his horn against your husband, and stand in your son's stead. Well done, Sarah! This is a joke for all creation to savor. A ram from God!"

A puff of wind on Sarah's cheek, laughter in the distance, and soon, Sarah saw, the donkey had ceased its trembling. She mounted and they cantered on, Sarah spurring with her heels.

After a while she abandoned the donkey and went the rest of the way on foot, all the while reassuring herself. Isaac is young and Abraham old. If need be Isaac could topple that old man! But then she stumbled on thoughts hard as the stones of the mountain. Despair will rob Isaac of power. Make him submit to his father's force!

I raised a son to gentleness. Let it not kill him now.

She was late, too late! Isaac lay on the altar, his body bound with ropes, his face contorted in fear.

Sarah's cry of anguish so terrified the animal she carried that it smashed through the sack and charged into a thicket where it snared its horns, and was caught.

As was Abraham, mid-murder, the slaughterer's knife raised over his son.

Abraham's body was sweat-drenched, his knife-wielding fist shook with power. He could not change course. God had to send two angels to hang on his arm and drag it down.

"Abraham!" they cried, entering the episode at last. "Here is a ram for slaughter. No need to kill Isaac! Put an end to this shameful scene!"

Abraham looked wildly around for God, but saw only his wife clutching her breast. He scowled at her with all the fear and confusion in his own heart. Then with slow fingers he untied Isaac.

Sarah dragged herself from that place. Once she reached

home, all the jagged stones she carried in her heart—the journey, the meeting with God, the sight of Isaac trussed on the altar like an animal for killing—crushed her with their weight. Sarah died, never to see Isaac again.

God lengthened the last of Sarah's earthly moments in hope of some final witticism to lighten his ever-darkening mood. Under the circumstances, the best Sarah could come up with was this:

"You made time slow for me, God, as I hurried toward Isaac's rescue. Now time rushes me toward rescue from all but You."

She heard laughter at her ear, felt embraced and lifted toward light. At the same moment, she knew that the God she talked and laughed with was no more than a merciful illusion God had laid across the darkness that separated them. She would reach beyond the illusion only when life had left her.

With her last breaths she uttered three piercing cries. Those who witnessed her death thought, "Sarah has flung her cries into the abyss of unknowing as Zipporah flung the foreskin of Moses' child at the pursuing God! Sarah's cries are as sharp as circumcision! They will be our inheritance, we will hear them whenever we hurl anguish or hope into the stony ear of the ram's horn."

Tekiah: "Whoooooooooooooooo-*ooo!*"

Shevarim: "Are-you; are-you; are-you; are-you!"

Teruah: "Are you-you-you-you-you-you-you-you!"

And what of the answers? Ah, they thought, answers come as coded as the cries! Sometimes warm and near, or from great, cold distances . . . faint . . . fainter. They thought of these things as they prepared for burial the body of the Matriarch, Sarah. Who can tell, they wondered, whether silence is a degree of speech we have not yet learned to fathom?

REBEKAH

GENESIS 27:1–13

When Isaac was old and his eyes were too dim to see, he called his older son Esau and said to him, "My son." He answered, "Here I am." And he said, "I am old now, and I do not know how soon I may die. Take your quiver and bow and go out into the open and hunt some game. Then prepare a dish for me such as I like, and bring it to me to eat, so that I may give you my innermost blessing before I die."

Rebekah had been listening as Isaac spoke to his son Esau. When Esau had gone out into the open to hunt game to bring home, Rebekah said to her son Jacob, "I overheard your father speaking to your brother Esau, saying, 'Bring me some game and prepare a dish for me to eat, that I may bless you, with the Lord's approval, before I die.' Now, my son, listen carefully as I instruct you. Go to the flock and fetch me two choice kids, and I will make of them a dish for your father, such as he likes. Then take it to your father to eat, in order that he may bless you before he dies. Jacob answered his mother Rebekah, "But my brother Esau is a hairy man and I am smooth-skinned. If my father touches me, I shall appear to him as a trickster and bring upon myself a curse, not a blessing." But his mother said to him, "Your curse, my son, be upon me! Just do as I say and go fetch them for me."

COMMENTARY

On the long journey back to Canaan, Abraham's messenger, having once before turned eloquent, rouses himself to lighten time for Rebekah. He recites a version of the story he told her family after the meeting at the well.

"What good luck for you, Rebekah! Your future is assured. Abraham is your wise and powerful father-in-law. He smashed the old idols. True God spoke to him: 'Take your son and sacrifice him on the mountain. . . .' "

But before this part of Eliezer's story can reach Rebekah's hearing, a strong desert wind rises up in the space between the messenger's mouth and Rebekah's ear and blows the words away. When the messenger realizes what has happened, he sprints to another part of the story: "And what bad luck for you, Rebekah, that you couldn't know Sarah! A woman of courage, a beauty in her day. God also spoke to her. God personally announced to Sarah the birth of Isaac, your husband! Marvelous family. Lucky girl, Rebekah! Watch out for those sinkholes—just nudge your camel a little that way."

He speaks to a servant as he rides away, "God does not yet want her to know that Abraham nearly sacrificed her husband."

But the servant resolves to tell her himself. "Here's a story," he says, riding alongside Rebekah. "There were two brothers; they had a hard life. One, a boy, barely 14, was barred from the house. His father sent him into the wilderness. Do you think any human creature came with a drop of water? God did. Miracle! Then this same father raised his hand to kill the second son. Don't ask me to explain, but this boy, too, was saved at the last minute. A miracle he's still alive, your . . ."

As the servant pronounces Isaac's name, all the camels in the caravan set up a loud braying and drown out the word. What Rebekah hears is "Br-r-ra-a-a-ak!" In fear, the servant rides quickly away. "God does not want the darkness of Isaac's fear to fill her mind," he says to the other servants.

Then Rebekah's nurse and maids ride to her side. They try to speak of what they've learned on the way. But Rebekah's brother had warned, "Don't chatter on the journey, as women do! Don't pester the messenger with questions. He's told his story. Remember he comes from God, at least from Abraham's God. Keep your face veiled, your eyes on your camel, and whatever you do, don't disgrace your family!" Rebekah silences her maids. "It is the image of the bold and forthright messenger Eliezer," they reflect, "that lures our mistress toward Isaac. Better that she not know the truth, lest she balk at God's plan."

Thus the caravan travels in silence, respectful of the journeying bride, her ignorance, her fear, her longing, her sacred mission. Of that mission she knows only that water, and the simple daily task of drawing from the well, have washed away all that she possessed of home. And so Rebekah remains ignorant of the *Akedah,* the binding of Isaac, the man she is to marry.

When at last she beholds the anxious figure of Isaac,

nervously pacing in a field, she falls from her camel in a faint. Before she is fully restored to herself, Isaac carries her into his dead mother's tent to seal their marriage.

"What has been hidden," say the messenger, the servant, the nurse, and the maids, "God will make known to Rebekah."

The passage above is an invention in the manner of traditional midrash, a form of Bible commentary written by rabbis in the first centuries of the Common Era. Midrash asks questions about gaps or other difficulties that appear in Bible stories and sometimes invents answers to account for them. The midrash I have written asks a question about a striking gap in the Bible story of Rebekah—does no one ever tell her about the *Akedah,* the binding and near-sacrifice of Isaac by his father?—and supplies an imagined text to account for the not-telling.

Other aspects of the Rebekah and Isaac story are also, in my view, prime midrashic moments, spaces in the story to be questioned, elucidated, imagined. Yet I do not find them among examples of midrashic literature. The Bible itself recounts only the end of Rebekah's journey to meet the husband she has never seen. Eliezer, the messenger, identifies the figure of Isaac in a field. Rebekah descends (or falls) from the camel. Isaac approaches.

Though much is made of the ceremony of drawing and offering water when Eliezer first meets Rebekah at the well, here at Rebekah's first encounter with Isaac, no water is mentioned. There is only the messenger's summary to Isaac of "all the things he had done," with their implied confirmation of Rebekah's credentials, and Isaac's precipitous taking of Rebekah into the deceased Sarah's tent, where he is "comforted after his mother" (Genesis 24:67). And that is all. No water, no refreshment. "What ceremony else?" one longs to ask, as Hamlet does over Ophelia's grave.

Traditional midrash does not address an ironic absence here, though to me the text cries out for it. Why, when Isaac greets his bride, is there no mention of the element in which the earlier text is drenched? In this lack, this obliviousness to Rebekah's needs, accompanied by Isaac's thirst for instant sexual gratification for himself, aren't we meant to understand that for Rebekah a dry, infertile period will follow? In fact, Rebekah is barren for the first 20 years of her marriage to Isaac.

The journey midrash I have invented accounts for Rebekah's not knowing an all-important fact about her husband, but it leaves her much as the rabbis found her, passing from her father's to her husband's house in passive acquiescence to her own ignorance. We are left with an astonishing mystery: How did Rebekah become a woman capable of acting according to her own mind, of deceiving her husband, and imposing her view of covenantal succession on husband and sons?

How, in fact, did Rebekah respond to her 20 years of barrenness in a time when having children (sons, biblical women always said) was a woman's raison d'être? We know how decisively, if despotically, Sarah responded to a similar affliction: She gave her handmaid Hagar as concubine to Abraham; when she herself conceived a son she banished the handmaid with the handmaid's son, Ishmael, even if it meant their death. It is the voice of God itself that creates the midrash for Sarah's act: God tells Abraham that Sarah is right, covenantal succession will depend on Isaac, not Ishmael, and that God will provide for Ishmael, too.

But how did *Rebekah* respond to barrenness? And what was the effect on Rebekah of becoming the wife of a man whose father had been willing to kill him as a sacrifice to God? Might not these aspects of Rebekah's married life have contributed to the forging of her astonishing plan to rearrange the order in which her sons, Jacob and Esau, receive their father's blessing, and to her ability to carry out that plan?

Bible and midrash alike are silent. The rabbis imagined much but never, so far as I can tell, conjectured about the effect of the *Akedah* or of the 20 barren years on Rebekah's decisions and acts. Perhaps more centuries had to pass before even such close readers as the ancient rabbis could have perceived those spaces in a story whose elements are, to adapt Auerbach's rendering in terseness: the well, the tent, the barrenness, the twins, the deception.

Midrash can help us trace the heroic development of a woman who began in virginal submissiveness and transformed herself into an autonomous individual, clear-sighted and courageous enough to see—and act—beyond her husband's purview.

I have imagined for Rebekah a response to the *Akedah* and to barrenness. Not, as in Sarah's case, by supplying another woman's womb to her husband, but by seeking another source of seed for herself. This midrash may seem to some readers to be far from the restrictive conventions for women of biblical times, as indeed in some sense it is; in another sense we can say that no contemporary act could be bolder than the one this biblical woman has already shown herself capable of, the wresting of the patriarch's blessing from the first-born son to the second.

Then and now are divided by what is permitted sexually to a woman. Here, where the rabbis refused to conjecture, we can move further into modernity with a midrash that suggests the rebellious, then *autonomous*, woman Rebekah became. Having found no existing midrash to reflect my questions, and certainly none to answer them, I undertook to write "Rebekah and Isaac: A Marriage Made in Heaven."

Rebekah and Isaac: A Marriage Made in Heaven

After the excitement at the well, drawing water for the messenger, his camels; after gifts of gold, arm-bangle, nose-ring; after Isaac's lovemaking in his mother's tent, Sarah, who had died, I began to look about, amazed, at marriage.

I asked my maids to tell about this bridegroom—the truth, whether I liked it or not—who was so nervous, something always on his mind. What could it be, what had they heard?

They thought it safe to tell me then, like it or not: the knife at Isaac's neck, rods beneath him ready for flame, poor Yitzhak trussed for burning.

"Nightsweats, heart-sinks, black mopes! That's the fun your husband had in life. Feel sorry for him," they said. "He had a dreadful youth. Went out with Abraham one day and saw his father prepare to kill him. And would have—you know Abraham!—if there'd been no ram! Since that unfathomed day, sudden death is Isaac's fear. So at the mere approach of you, my dear (maybe he's got to finish things as quick as can!), well—need we spell it out? Because of that you won't conceive, a sin the family expects you'll take upon yourself. And we must call you barren woman."

They said I'd learn to live with it, like it or not. Sorry for me but no stopping now. What's kept in comes out, and always that way, ancient or modern.

"No one bothered to tell you the family troubles. Now you know Abraham tried to kill Isaac at God's command. And what a comedy of errors killed Isaac's mother! Fitting, really, since at God's announcement of her pregnancy, Sarah laughed. Then, when the messenger came with news—'Abraham lifted his knife to slay your son, but Isaac is spared from death!'—she heard only the first part and dropped dead before clause two. Because of that you never met your mother-in-law. Though what sort of relative could Sarah be to you—late-in-life mother, overprotective, yet in the end unable to save her son?

"Don't you know that you were chosen?" my women asked. "You're married to a survivor, like it or not, imprinted deeper with our destiny than most."

They gossiped on, all secrets out, and whispered of a banished brother whose name itself was sibilant as secrets. "Ish-sh-sh-mael!" A daring, forthright man. The kind, they said, I must have dreamed I'd marry, led on camelback toward Isaac by the gold-bestowing messenger.

"No man of course takes concubines for pleasure!" They broadly winked among themselves. "So Abraham in piety took Hagar, since barrenness was Sarah's portion. Strictly for conception—and at Sarah's urge!—for pious reasons only.

Hagar might conceive a child, and did. Ishmael—it's Ishmael!"

"Why does God withhold from us?" I asked my husband.

"You call this 20-year trifle a withholding? My mother had to wait till 90, my father till 100 years to have me!"

"Are we like them?" I asked.

"When we traveled through the desert once, do you remember how I claimed you were my sister? Abraham did that with my mother, too. I had to see if God would speak with miracles, close for me the wombs of Pharaoh's women as he did for Abraham, should anyone dare touch you. God gave me answer. Unstained! You were unstained!"

I shuddered in remembrance of that journey. Answers felt like life or death to me. "*Are* we like Abraham and Sarah?"

I pray I'm like my father," Isaac said, "yet dread it. I wait to see if God will strike me as he struck at Abraham. Sometimes I think God's mercy stops your bearing because of what I, too, would have to bear. The call to Mount Moriah! Once sacrificed, to be the sacrificer would be jeopardy of agonizing doubleness. Yet dreams already lead me there. I mount the path. My son's beside me. I feel again how all my bones turn liquid. When Abraham bound *me!* All but pierced *my* throat . . . !"

"Isaac, don't relive that nightmare time! You're safe, and in my arms!" Dread fell on me. But Isaac, like so many who stay silent, when confession's mode is on him, can't rest until the end.

"My arm goes limp, I tell you, too weak to wield a knife!

I am unable to fulfill God's will! And there's no ram and no redemption. Only ashes from which nothing can rise!"

At that they say I let out piercing screams, and fell in a faint, as Sarah did. I pity her, who never rose again. *But I will not be like her!*

I see that I, too, wait for repetition. "How like Sarah you are!" the people say. Why should I pray to have a son if he's a sacrifice? Yet not sacrificed, of course, but saved! And therefore doubly precious! Yet shocked into lifelong dread, and I like Sarah will die of it! Or maybe . . . what Isaac fears will happen? The botched call to faith, followed by shame and death!

I argue with sick thoughts. Why need this go exactly as with Abraham? Yet the voice of fear returns: Suppose God's test is meant to come in every generation? Then God must *vary* the results! Isaac might do all that's needed and *still* our son be doomed!

I am resolved. When the stealthy messenger arrives, I'll be alert for news. I'll intervene and go in Isaac's place, without my son. Up the mountain! Lay myself on dry sticks! Let God's angels slit my throat and light the fire, or let me go. And declare at last that we are chosen not for death but life!

I've made my plan. I keep my spirits up. I'm ready to laugh at a moment's notice should the angel of birth appear to say, "You'll bear a son!"

No messenger approaches me with good news or Isaac with the bad. I haven't caught him listening in the night. I haven't caught myself in laughter yet.

"Be patient," Isaac says. "Till God, remembering Sarah, fills your womb."

But what if God should vary these trials, too? My child's by no means guaranteed! I will not be like Sarah!

With scrawled address in hand (my women are as sharp as private eyes) I went in search of Hagar. And found her in a place not wholly hovel.

"How do you manage?" I asked in sympathy, thinking how my Isaac, despite all faults, is such a good provider. I saw too late that I had scratched her pride.

"Abraham," said Hagar, "sends regular contributions. Neighbors have assisted, too, though more for their own comfort than for ours. But that will all soon end."

"It's right to do mitzvot," I said, and reached for pocket-shekels. Hagar raised an intercepting palm. "No charity from you! My son has expectations!"

She'd mentioned Ishmael first. That seemed to me a sign, and gave me courage. "May I speak of painful matters—how Sarah cast him out . . .?"

"Who never should have left!" cried Hagar. " 'Cast out Sarah with Isaac, *her* son,' I said to Abraham. 'Honor your first-born!'

"Ah, how he tried, poor man, to clear the way for Ishmael! Jousting with God, quibbling for definitions, searching for ways to forestall. 'Only son?' said Abraham to God. 'Who's my only son? I've two! The one I love? I love them both!' One other way he tried I'd shudder to speak of."

"I know it now," I said.

"God saw my son and me cast out and dying, and sent

water, angels, anything we wanted! Behind the driest thicket, springs of water!"

That day still raged in Hagar. Carefully, I chose my words. "Ishmael should be restored to Abraham's house, now Sarah's dead. And you be honored as well. Believe me, Hagar, I know justice is as greatly owed to you as Ishmael! As for me, I am deprived of mother-in-law and mother, and of a child, year after year! You've borne a son. But does that keep you from consideration of a daughter's dangers?"

I felt ringed with dangers, yet calm. All seemed ordained. My caution vanished. I was impelled, pulled, called! As if the world's last chance for offspring rested with me! The courage of Lot's daughters was no more than mine. Maybe my foolhardiness was like theirs, too. Still—God loves daring. Yet we earn God's wrath if we presume too much. Our tragedy is that "much" and "little" are defined not by our own perspective but by God's great sight. We see too late, our acts beyond recall. I had no choice but press my cause.

"Since men have spouses and concubines—Hagar, please don't be offended!—then why can't women have both? By taking very little trouble, lines of inheritance could be determined, as they are with men. . . .

"It is not with women as it is with men!" said Hagar strictly.

"Yes, yes, that's true—we don't, as men do, strew our seed so wastefully. But women sometimes suffer barrenness—who, more than you, has witnessed with more triumph? Perhaps an alternate, coming to the tent at night, could cure that cursed condition?"

I will not be like Sarah, I vowed. I will not wait for 90

years, nor let my son be taken! Before me stands the woman I emulate!

"Hagar," I cried, "come live in Abraham's house! Be mother to motherless Isaac and me! Bring Ishmael with you to father our sons. I know my powers of persuasion, I can arrange it!"

"God is great," said Hagar. "No one suffers for nothing. Once I cried for concubines' crumbs. Now my son will be father of a great nation! That promise God gave as freely as the drink of water in the wilderness when we lay parched. As for my return to Abraham's house, that would do for me as wife, not less. No more of being concubines! I speak from experience of the condition. How I remember Sarah's taunts! Now my son will be father of a great nation. It's promised! No, one doesn't suffer for nothing. No second best for us, never again! No sneaking under the shield of Abraham's covenant. We have our own! Ishmael to be father of a great nation!"

This concubine had beauty, still. And strength, a resoluteness high as Abraham's. She drew my soul in admiration. Here was a mother—not like Sarah!—whose cries and prayers had saved her child! But Hagar turned on me rage that had seethed till now.

"It's not *my* son who'll swap God's promise for a meal, however succulent your porridge, however guilefully you offer it! I'll see that Ishmael knows better than demean himself with you, and I forbid return except to see his father buried, as is right. Keep your history separate from me and mine. I scorn your triumphs, as God forbid I'd have to share your fall!"

Women look about them after marriage. Like it or not, like Emma Bovary, that romance-craving wife, they pine. No one told me anything before my journey. Yet my body feels the agony of Sarah, who was—God help me!—barren till old age. She met with bitter laughter God's foretelling she'd give birth. Then, humbled, gave her son the name of Yizhak, laughter, giving God last laugh. Laugh and laughed-at turn about and go on sporting with each other till our death.

My women, no less crafty at procuring, like it or not, than Cleopatra's were, brought brawny Ishmael to my tent. He was every inch as much as Isaac Abraham's son, maybe by several inches more so. I was in good shape, too: My arms had lifted water from a well.

"How midrash will malign you, Ishmael, call you brutish lout! Midrash, the apologetic sort, says you aimed arrows at the passing folk, and made your overtures of sex to little Isaac. Sarah banished you with Hagar. Yet we know where Sarah's arrow aimed: inheritance for Isaac! If I'm to pity, why not pity you, cast out by Isaac's mother with your own, then saved from death by miracle as great as spared my husband? Yet the horror doesn't scar *your* psyche! Mother-in-law I never saw put you off limits, as if your manhood were a spindle for Isaac's pricking on. Well—Sleeping Beauty's found you. Prick! And ghost of mother-in-law be banished!"

Ishmael exulted: "Now I chisel out my fate! *Me* will your son resemble!" Here was God's message—Ishmael, maker of sons. But before we could be known to one another in my tent, thunder boomed, lightning glared, hailstones battered down the roof! Drenched, lit up like day, beaten by hail whose aim was true as arrows, Ishmael cried, "Sarah scourges me still!" and fled. After that, Isaac came to bed full-strength, inspired by I know not what, nor dare to think about.

In the same hour I bore Ishmael-like Esau and Isaac-like Jacob. They split between them again, like my husband and his brother, fear and trembling on one side, heartiness on the other. Right then I swore to alter balances, set heritance on hardihood, not nerves. Isaac, himself, poor self-despiser, hankered to swagger on in Esau's genes!

But from deep within the well between my thighs where destiny awaited ladling out, I chose the child that Isaac didn't (like it or not, a common marriage story), yet chose the child most like my spouse! Clapped bracelet-pelts on hairless Jacob's arm, and led him by that nose ring, mother love, to fool his father.

I'd told my sons what Isaac suffered at *his* father's hand. I don't believe in keeping things from children. "It's quite all right to act this way," I said. "Not only is your father blind, he's also had to turn deaf ears to God for fear of what God's voice might say. He just can't hear the choice of heir God urged him toward. It's up to us to make interpretations. I always wanted you to share, and get along. Remember everyone gets something, more or less. I hope you'll make me proud and be good sports about it. Since we're clearly actors in God's play, let's make the best of all our roles. If it's to weep, we'll do so; if to exult, we must with all our might. Above all not draw back from what's ordained.

And so I fooled blind, dying Isaac into glory, which

consists, at least in part, of getting yourself written into the right story. Then, cradling my old husband in my arms, I lulled his way to rest with our old made-in-heaven song. The well, the tent, the twins, the blessing, I sang.

"Look," I urged into his white-blind eyes, "look at the lengths to which the Holy One goes, for—like it not or like it—us."

RACHEL AND LEAH

GENESIS 29:14–30

When he had stayed with him a month's time, Laban said to Jacob, "Just because you are a kinsman, should you serve me for nothing? Tell me, what shall your wages be?" Now Laban had two daughters; the name of the older one was Leah, and the name of the younger was Rachel. Leah had weak eyes; Rachel was shapely and beautiful. Jacob loved Rachel; so he answered, "I will serve you seven years for your younger daughter Rachel." Laban said, "Better that I give her to you than that I should give her to an outsider. Stay with me." So Jacob served seven years for Rachel and they seemed to him but a few days because of his love for her.

Then Jacob said to Laban, "Give me my wife, for my time is fulfilled, that I may cohabit with her." And Laban gathered all the people of the place and made a feast. When evening came, he took his daughter Leah and brought her to him; and he cohabited with her. . . . When morning came, there was Leah! So he said to Laban, "What is this you have done to me? I was in your service for Rachel! Why did you deceive me?" Laban said, "It is not the practice in our place to marry off the younger before the older. Wait until the bridal week of this one is over and we will give you that one, too, provided you serve me another seven years." Jacob did so; he waited out the bridal week of the one, and then he gave him his daughter Rachel as wife. . . . And Jacob cohabited with Rachel also; indeed, he loved Rachel more than Leah. And he served him another seven years.

COMMENTARY

The scandal of two sisters who—how else can we put this?—sleep with the same man, names the notoriety of Rachel and Leah. Later this arrangement is forbidden by *halakhah,* but for the space of the Bible story it is mightily in force. Rachel is a beauty, the one desired by Jacob. Leah is "weak-eyed," generally understood to mean that her whole self was without the luster of sexual appeal. Whatever competitiveness existed between the sisters before Jacob came on the scene must have been greatly exacerbated by their sharing of a husband who loved one and despised the other.

Trickery taints the tale. Laban, father of the sisters, tricks Jacob into taking Leah as wife when Jacob thinks he is taking Rachel. The midrashists (in *Lamentations Rabba*) tell us that so great was the beautiful sister's pity for her ugly sister that Rachel lay beneath the wedding couch all night after Leah's marriage to Jacob, responding to Jacob's lovemaking in her own voice so that Jacob, deceived, would not stint in lovemaking to Leah.

Jacob, in turn, deceives Laban in the matter of the livestock he is entitled to, and Rachel caps the whole adventure by stealing her father's household idols. After Jacob leaves Laban's house he encounters Esau, whom he had deceived and cheated out of his birthright.

Laban and Esau are left behind, but the sister-wives at the center of Jacob's life continue the Bible story by rivalrously competing in baby-bearing.

The midrashic rabbis, however, struck a note of compassion and transcendence when they invented the somewhat scandalous, somewhat comically scabrous, but nonetheless humane and moving wedding night of Leah, the unloved. On that night, Rachel hid herself beneath the bed. So that her sister might not be shamed, before her bridal night was over, by Jacob's discovery that he had been tricked into sleeping with Leah, Rachel lent her voice to her sister, sympathetically breathing up love notes from below.

Those are the notes I take up, extend, and embellish in the midrash, "Rachel and Leah: A Thousand and One Nights of Love."

Rachel and Leah: A Thousand and One Nights of Love

On the thousand-and-first night of lovemaking, Jacob the Patriarch bathed his body in a stream.

His servant stood on the bank, holding Jacob's clothing and looking over certain tokens he kept to jog memory. The servant's name was Switchel, which in the old tongue means "changing." He kept the record of the women's days, and of who took which turn in Jacob's bed. After some muttering to himself, Switchel spoke. "Tonight," he said, "it will be Rachel."

"Ah!" Jacob's sigh was half pleasure, half groan. "This sisterhood of wives, Switchel! Foolishness, perhaps, to feel this way, since they're entirely devoted to me. But deep family feeling binds them. So deep, in fact, that on my wedding night Rachel concealed from me that Leah was thrust between my sheets by their trickster father!"

The servant looked up from his calculations and filled his voice with piety. "By this, we see the devotion of my mistress Rachel. She wished to help her sister survive that difficult night, and equally to assure her husband the greatest pleasure, having seen that you preferred to bed with her."

Jacob cast a shrewd glance at the servant. He suspected him of being in the pay of one or both of his wives. Yet he liked the skill of the man in praising virtue. He comforted himself: Everything no doubt has been as Switchel described it. And so Jacob prepared to lie with his beloved wife, Rachel, for what the servant assured him would be their thousand-and-first night of love.

In Leah's tent, the sisters are busy at the work of preparing for love, though only one of them with zeal. Leah sits dispirited on a stool. Rachel, alert with the loveliness of the loved, moves with assurance through her preparations.

"You must apply this scent to your armpits, Leah," Rachel says. "The animal from which it is extracted draws the male to her rump as surely as you will draw Jacob to your embrace."

Leah's gown sags off one bony shoulder. A belt of woven flax is wound around her middle which is as slim as Rachel's, but it does not sit well there, as the same sash does on Rachel's gown. There is something baggy and ill-formed about the whole of Leah's outfit, as if well-being, that mysterious essence that plumps up the fit of everything, has seeped through the seams.

"It's no use, Rachel. I've given up these potions. Nothing will draw Jacob to me except his servant's record of days and nights. To breed he will take me. Never for love. I know the difference. I have been a thief of his love on those nights when he believed I was you. He will have been robbed and not known it for 1,000 nights."

"A good thing, too!" Rachel smoothes lotion onto the skin of her sister's bare shoulder.

At a new thought Leah lifts her head. "Is it hatred of Jacob that makes you destroy his pleasure?"

"I never hated Jacob. But surely you see how bad it is for a man to dictate every moment of the marriage bed. I determined that much on the long night I lay beneath yours."

"When our father tossed me like counterfeit coin into Jacob's bed, you lay beneath, and in the dark, lent me your voice. It was not until morning that Jacob detected me, despised usurper of his seed. And you and I have continued so throughout the years. . . ."

Rachel laughs at the thought of it. "It's true! When Jacob wants Rachel, Rachel sends in Leah. When Jacob asks for Leah, Leah sends in Rachel. Our modesty, of course, insists on darkness. In the morning, enjoying the joke that only you and I, and sometimes Switchel, can, we ask one another: 'Was Jacob fervent with Rachel?' 'Was he cold to Leah?' "

Leah laughs loudly. But she lapses once more into melancholy. "When Jacob wakes in waxlight and we have gone, does he despair? Does he wonder, 'Could this have been Leah where I thought Rachel? Rachel where I thought Leah?' Is it your wish, Rachel, or is it good, that a man should be so confused in his marriage bed?"

"Are you so convinced of the good of things when he is not?"

Leah stands up suddenly. "I want to stop this masquerading! It doesn't make me feel better. It's a matter of time, anyway, before we're discovered. They will say we've gone back to our pagan roots."

"Stop masquerading? How, when it's the very center of married life! Leah, ours is important work! We inquire into the nature of reality, of sexuality, of marriage, of the springs of self-esteem, of the mystery of personality, of free will, of the covenant between God and woman, and probably other things was well I haven't thought of yet! Stop all that? How can you think of it!"

"That's a long list of accomplishments to come out of sleeping with a man who thinks I'm dirt. I can't see what's in this for me, Rachel, except maybe revenge, but that wears very thin." Leah's voice is weary. "Tonight's the thousand-and-first night of our deception, I asked Switchel. It's time to quit unless you can convince me otherwise before Jacob's bedtime."

Rachel makes a few friendly passes at Leah's stringy hair, cocking her head this way and that, and smiling, as if she sees some great improvement in whether a strand lies down or across.

"I will take up your challenge, Leah. I will convince you of the need to continue. I will do it while I arrange you hair and your ornaments, and you and I will still have time to share a cup of wine before our husband's summons."

Leah pulls up one knee with her hands and slumps into a listening posture. "Don't make it too complicated. If we're going through with this tonight, I still have to keep my wits about me in Jacob's bed. If you are discovered, it's: 'Welcome,

Rachel!' If I am, it's: 'Get her out of here!' I have to work harder than you at my disguise."

"I understand, and will keep to my points." Rachel takes up a fresh comb. Studying her sister's head as if planning her strategy, she begins to speak in a contemplative tone.

"Should Jacob never know when his passion will have its way? Yes, absolutely. That is good! Good to dilute the arrogance of desire. Jacob, who wants to command his choice, can no longer choose, but be chosen. Each night, whenever possible, he is chosen by a woman not of his choice. In this way we force his unfortunately narrow nature to expand. He has no choice but to widen. He must receive the woman who comes to him as he would receive a stranger-guest who might be an angel of God. He prepares for this woman, who is unknown to him, his choicest feast. She may, after all, *be* his choice."

"Leah interrupts impatiently. "He thinks we are who we aren't! How does that widen anything except the gap between truth and deception? Or are you saying, Rachel, that you think Jacob already suspects our fraud? And would Jacob think this a good thing, too, if he knew?"

"I will answer you this way," says Rachel. "Until Jacob can perceive that this is good, he is no fit judge of the good."

"I, who am despised, will tell you what I know of human love! It's how we come closest to love of God. Jacob, who was once gripped by an angel, must feel that love through you."

"A beginning needn't be an end. Can't we go through love of one to love of many? God has more aspects than any single earthly love can make us understand. And therefore, when I'm dead . . ."

"Don't! This life may be suffering, but I never like to speak of dying."

"All the same, when I'm dead and see the suffering of our people, I won't distinguish among those I've loved or haven't. My pity will embrace them all if it's to be any use in catching God's compassion."

Bathing his body in the stream, murmuring half to himself, half to his servant, Switchel, Jacob the Patriarch said, "My wretched father-in-law, with his double daughters! Rachel and Leah! Leah and Rachel! He set this pattern of confounding my senses. 'I'll work my seven years for Rachel, your beautiful younger daughter, whom I love,' I told the father. 'Yes, yes, of course,' the old scoundrel said. And then on my wedding night he put his ugly daughter in my bed. I had to breed with her a full week before I could plough through to my darling, and then work another seven years to win what I'd been promised in the first place. The memory of it eats at me unceasingly."

"You were shamefully treated!"

Jacob climbed onto the bank, naked and dripping, a handsome, smooth-skinned man. A slight limp gave him the romantic air of an adventurer, though he was in fact a cautious man. He dried himself with the rough-woven cloth the servant handed him. As he rubbed his chest, he looked into the distance, where the last streaks of evening bloodied the sky.

"I myself confounded my father's trust, surely you've heard the story? I posed as his elder son, Esau, to usurp the first-born's blessing. People still whisper of it, I suppose."

"Ah, is that so?" Switchel assumed an innocent air. "No, I hadn't heard. You really mustn't let your sensitive feelings lead you to imagine things!"

"There is a certain wit in twosomes, all the same," Jacob went on meditatively. "One must salute it. Things have a way of doubling back. Water reflects sky and sky echoes water. Wombs are twinned, yet carry only one inheritor of the covenant. This is the mystery of our creation. We long for the One. Yet the simplicity of one eludes us."

"Indeed, how true!" responded Switchel, whose purse was filling up so satisfactorily with coins the trickster sisters paid him. "How very true that the multiplications of matter quite steal away our singleness of purpose."

Rachel brushes out a bang on her sister's forehead.

"You must admit, Leah, that there is interest and playfulness to our lives because we are two. We avoid marital staleness. We are not limited to a single life or even to a single husband, since Jacob is a different man with me when he thinks me Rachel and when he thinks me Leah. And Jacob is two husbands for you—when he is with you as Leah and you as Rachel. Think of it! I know what it is to be Leah—that is extraordinary!"

"I know what it is to be Rachel. But it's bitter to be Rachel when I know I'm only Leah."

Rachel stares at her sister in astonishment. "But you *are* Rachel when you are being Rachel! I am Leah when I am being Leah. And the proof of it is, when I am Leah, Leah is nowhere else. When I am Leah, where is Leah? She is in Jacob's bed, despised, coldly treated, quickly dispatched, thrust away. I am Leah and I suffer my husband's cruelty, and I say to myself, 'I will remember you, Jacob, I will remember who you are. Not my gentle lover, but crude! Selfish. Brutal. Thoughtless self-gratifier. I will remember, Jacob, that you are Esau!' "

"Oh. Is that who he is?" Leah winces under her sister's energetic comb.

"And where are *you,* then, Leah? In your tent you are not despised and coldly treated as I, Leah, am in Jacob's bed. No, you are desired, longed-for, loved in your absence, sent passionate thoughts that rush at your bed like fierce angels. You are then more truly Rachel than I."

"Clever sister, you make my head spin. There is enjoyment for you in this game of substitution that there never can be for me. Regardless of your words that tell me I am you and you are I, I feel my own self still hang about my neck. If our game should ever end, I will be cast down again to Leah, while you will still be Rachel."

"Then may the game never end. Give me your sons, Leah. You shall have mine. Let us exchange them in our hearts. Who knows but that Reuben, conceived in you by Jacob thinking you Rachel, and Joseph, conceived in me by Jacob thinking me Leah, may more truly be our joint sons than we have realized."

"Then must my loyalty, Rachel, be greater in all things to you than to my husband? I have not quite taken that in."

"Yes! As mine must be to you. As the loyalty of our husband's mother, Rebekah, was greater toward her son than to *her* husband. Let us not allow this man, this Jacob, this husband, to come between us. His spirit was divided at his own birth, half of it carried off by his twin. Had Jacob shown love to his brother, Esau, as you and I have done as sisters, we should be hearing a different story now from the world."

"Our own sons are already influenced by Jacob's strong desires," says Leah. "They want to prefer and scorn as he does."

"We must work harder at our task! Spin the wheel! Disguise identity until reality itself grows dizzy! Have and have not. Be and yet not be. Yours and mine. Will and will not. Desire and despise."

"We are two, Rachel. We can never be one. We were two little girls in our father's house, and now we are two women in our husband's. That is God's truth."

"Of course that is the truth, Leah. We are two, our lives bound together. One will not prosper without the other."

Rachel summons a servant. "Tell your master, Jacob, 'Rachel is not well. Leah will come tonight in her stead.' "

Leah turns to stare at her sister. Rachel places a reassuring hand on her shoulder, and continues,

"And tell your master, further, these words: 'Though it may be that Rachel will recover and come as promised.' "

Leah's body sags with relief.

"And make sure," Rachel adds, "that you remind Switchel to darken the room for modesty's sake."

Jacob put on fresh robes. "How can I be sure these women don't switch their babies, too, Switchel, as well as themselves, eh? Can I be sure that Joseph my favorite is of Rachel?"

"Try not to be paranoid," the servant said, "just because they fooled you once."

"The experience of women is altering. I wrestled with the angel at Peniel, after which I walked with a different gait and a different name. But that was good, clean combat! Compared to this wrestling with two sister-wives . . ." Jacob broke off with another groan. "Between them they squeeze and pull and push my very marrow into another shape. What shape, I couldn't tell you yet, but I feel"—here Jacob began to stretch and groan again as if all his muscles ached—"I feel somehow a change is coming over me."

"His mother did it," says Leah, taking a long sip of wine and passing the cup to her sister.

"You're right about that," Rachel agrees. "His mother Rebekah spoiled Jacob by choosing him, giving him preference." She dips her face into the wine cup like a reader of fortunes. "Wives must undo the mischief of mothers."

"Who like to create sons in their own image," Leah adds.

"On the other hand, would we want Jacob to resemble his brother whom his mother didn't care for and *didn't* spoil? Esau, grunting for food? Poor man, what might he have been if his mother had loved him! No, a mother's devotion is needed for the civilizing of a son, that's clear. Jacob has his faults, but at least a few refinements. As mothers we have our obligation."

"It's a job and a half for any woman, to keep that balance with boys. And I'm already tired." Leah reaches for the wine.

"Luckily there are two of us to share the burden! Single-wife marriages cannot accomplish what we can."

"Still, sister," Leah argues, "we have often caused one another grief as well. I don't rebuke you, or myself. I only remind, as a question of truth. In the matter of sons, in the number of sons."

"Let us confound Jacob in this as well. Let us not keep from one another any potion or matter or method having to do with planning our parenthood."

Leah hesitates, then reaches into the bosom of her gown. "My son found mandrakes, said to lure desire, or cause fecundity, or God only knows what other claims are made for such things." Leah holds out a fistful of white-fleshed, man-shaped roots.

Rachel takes one of the mandrakes, flourishes it through the air with a magician's gesture, then stirs it into the wine and drinks. "Henceforth we will speak only of *our* sons. We will share in creation."

"Jacob is intent on preference, no matter what," Leah remembers, rooted to realism by her unfortunate looks. "He has a favorite son and a favorite wife."

"We will root out this habit of mind if we can. The pride that says, 'This is my favorite,' means to say, 'This is *mine!*' In our struggle with Jacob we give him a new name, He-Who-Is-Redeemed-By-Women. This unspoken name will be perceived by him bit by bit as he alters. Let us teach He-Who-Is-Redeemed-By-Women that there is no ownership, except by God. Let us teach him to love all creatures who come from God. Let us teach him to love what he does not think he loves. And let us teach him that the one who is beloved and the one who is not beloved are one, and that they meet and meet again until they truly become what they have always been. One."

The women pour the remainder of the wine over the candle to extinguish it. In the dark, they whisper briefly. Then one of them rises, and walks toward Jacob's tent.

Sisters and Daughters

MIRIAM

NUMBERS 12:4–15

Suddenly the Lord called to Moses, Aaron, and Miriam. "Come out, you three, to the Tent of Meeting." So the three of them went out. The Lord came down in a pillar of cloud, stopped at the entrance of the Tent, and called out, "Aaron and Miriam!" The two of them came forward; and He said, "Hear these My words: When a prophet of the Lord arises among you, I make myself known to him in a vision, I speak with him in a dream. Not so with my servant Moses; he is trusted throughout my household. With him I speak mouth to mouth, plainly and not in riddles, and he beholds the likeness of the Lord. How, then, did you not shrink from speaking against my servant Moses!" Still incensed with them, the Lord departed.

As the cloud withdrew from the Tent, there was Miriam, stricken with snow-white scales. When Aaron turned toward Miriam, he saw that she was stricken with scales. And Aaron said to Moses, "Oh, my lord, account not to us the sin which we committed in our folly. Let her not be as one dead, who emerges from his mother's womb with half his flesh eaten away." So Moses cried out to the Lord, saying, "O God, pray heal her!"

But the Lord said to Moses, "If her father spat in her face, would she not bear her shame for seven days? Let her be shut out of camp for seven days, and then let her be readmitted." So Miriam was shut out of camp seven days; and the people did not march on until Miriam was readmitted.

COMMENTARY

Feminist readers make great claims for Miriam, sister of Moses. The Bible itself makes these claims for her: She is a prophet, a singer of victory at the Red Sea, savior of Moses and thus of the Hebrews first in Egypt and later, on the exodus from captivity. Without Miriam there would be no Moses, no exodus, no Jewish history.

Traditional midrash matches Miriam's life nearly miracle for miracle with that of Moses, though without crossing the line that would usurp Moses' power in favor of his sister's.

When Pharaoh decreed that first-born sons of the Hebrews should be killed, Miriam's father, in despair, refused to create more children. Miriam rebuked him for being harsher than Pharaoh. Traditional midrash thus adds to Miriam's honor responsibility for the very conception of Moses. The Bible story tells how Miriam saved Moses from death by floating him in his little boat down the Nile toward Pharaoh's daughter, and further ensuring his survival by putting forward his own mother as wet nurse. By the time the escaping Hebrews reached the Red Sea, Miriam has many times over earned her right to sing the victory song, "The horse and rider God has flung into the sea!"

During the arid and arduous journey toward Canaan, traditional midrash adds, it was Miriam's Well as much as the manna Moses prayed for that saved the people. Ginzberg's *The Legends of the Jews* tells us that water gushed up and followed them wherever they went. When the Hebrews made camp in the desert, the Well made an oasis that allowed fruit-bearing trees and herbs to grow, and grapes from which wine could be made. Like manna, the water of Miriam's Well could taste like anything—wine, honey, milk. Moreover, it had healing powers. Once a leper was healed by it—a poignant note, considering that Miriam's biblical punishment was to be stricken with leprosy.

When the midrashists address personal lives, they tell of Miriam's irritation with Moses. She, after all, receives prophecy just as Moses does, but she doesn't stop sleeping with her husband over it. Moses, on the other hand, according to his wife Zipporah's complaint (also recorded in Ginzberg's *The Legends of the Jews*), does not sleep with her while God is sending him messages. For rebuking Moses on this subject, Miriam and Aaron are both struck with leprosy, but only Miriam is also thrust outside the camp for seven days.

I have followed the lead of the classical midrashists in conflating time—not only vaulting contemporary over into ancient events, but also transposing Zipporah's mysterious foreskin-flinging encounter with God (Exodus 4:24–26) to a later place in Exodus. It occurs as an out-of-the-blue, timeless event in any case, unlinked to cause and effect in the narrative.

In the matter of that week of Miriam's expulsion from the camp, however, I have stayed true to linear biblical time, and have used it to form the basis of my own midrash, "The Seven Days of Miriam."

The Seven Days of Miriam

ON THE FIRST DAY, her mother and father came to see her in that shameful place. Not until she saw them could she weep. Until that moment she had lain on the ground without tears, without prayer, without hope or knowing. All as blank within as without. All motion and sound stopped, except her heart—its dull thuds, her breath—its useless search, in at her lips and out again, carrying no gift. Manna still fell for her, and they had left a jug of water. But in the arid landscape around her she daily read she was scorned, her powers gone, all the richness, energy, and imagination were for nothing, she had been slammed back against a brick wall with a mighty blow.

Her father and mother sat with her on the ground. "From the time you were small," her father said, "I knew your fearless ways would bring you a bad end. I smacked you but did it do any good? No—you had to get your smack from God. So now you know!"

Her mother brushed some dust from Miriam's robe. "Miriam, childsaver, I don't like to see you look so broken. I recognized your inventiveness as a child. Seven days of punishment by God is an honor, if you look at it in a certain way. As for this place outside where they've put you, Miriam, well, it's just like every place inside the camp. Don't you remember? Sagebrush, scorpions, lizards, days hot enough to fry manna on these rocks. Nights cold enough to freeze the hyena's laugh in its throat. I'm sure if your father stops to think about it he'll agree."

Miriam's father stopped to think. After a bit he said, reluctantly, "Well, I suppose, if you look at it in a certain way, you could say that in order for the punishment to be carried out, the whole of the Exodus had to stop. I mean, you weren't left behind, abandoned, which frankly I thought was going to happen. Imagine! All the people, stopped in their tracks and made to pitch their tents right there! The pillar of fire by night has to stay put, roaring in one fixed place like a tethered tornado. The pillar of cloud by day has to hang over everything, motionless, like a sinus headache. For seven days! And then there's your well, that was coming along with us, chugging through the earth like a monster mole, keeping its lid on so no dirt got inside, and then when we made camp, there it was, fresh water! Now it's sitting in one place just like the fire and the cloud. That's power, Miriam, there's no doubt about it. You're not being treated like some nobody with nothing to offer. I don't say I'm happy about this, but, now that I stop to think about it, maybe the family name isn't really smirched."

ON THE SECOND DAY, Moses visits Miriam. He weeps with her to see her brought so low.

She says, "You are my witness before God. I was a mother to you."

"Miriam, my sister and mother!"

She says, "Your cradle was to have been your grave. I made it into a life-barge instead. I led Pharaoh's daughter to your rescue."

"How many mothers I have had!"

She says, "I brought your own mother's breasts to your lips."

"How many mothers have I betrayed?"

She says, "Learn from my humiliation. You, too, will be cut off, the time will come. You won't see the promised land. I am a warning sacrifice. You will be cut off one day, too."

"Miriam, my sister and mother, my prophet! How many ways are there for God to speak! And how I love the silence of God!"

ON THE THIRD DAY, Miriam hears the approach of the elders. As they come toward her she sees a time when she will go down to a valley, to the deepest place of earth and her own soul, and receive God's laws there. When she comes back with the commandments, stitched as if by angels' fingers in gold and crimson and cerulean on sturdy woven cloth, decorated with leaves and flowers and fanciful birds' heads in flawless embroidery work, the men advance to take them from her.

"Too valuable," they say. "You might spill something on them—some blood, God forbid."

Miriam holds tight to the laws spelled out in beautiful brocaded letters.

"Besides, they're heavy, we're doing you a favor." The men tug, and wrest it from her arms.

"I held the baby Moses and never tired till I laid him in his cradle! Why are you doing this to me?"

"Moses will get them done in stone—strong! For the ages!"

"Stone will break! This will bend and last!"

"We think Moses should have them. His silence is more respectful than your comments. You're full of opinions. Having a stutterer lead us isn't a bad idea. The slower he speaks the less chance of arousing God's anger. Listen to you—you get in fifty words to his one. Between Moses the slow of speech and Miriam the firecracker is there a choice? It's a matter of community safety. You're inflammable material, Miriam. We're dousing you."

"But God spoke to me," Miriam screams.

"See? In two minutes she makes a commotion!"

"I call God to witness for me!"

"You know the story, Miriam. Once, there was an argument. Somebody said this, somebody else said that, and a third said, 'Let God make the synagogue walls slant in to prove I am right!' The synagogue walls did slant in, but nobody paid any attention because—do you understand this?—Torah is now on Earth! We interpret! We comment! We write down!"

"But the Heavenly Voice spoke to me!" says Miriam.

"Yes, yes, Heaven speaks and we hear. And we speak and Heaven hears. This is the concept. But between speaking and hearing, there is always room for interpretation. And we're it."

"Wait a minute!" says Miriam.

"Enough," they say, starting to move off.

Then Miriam does what she knows her father and her mother and Moses all wish she wouldn't do. She draws herself up, lowers her chin, pulls her brows together till they make a straight line over her frightening eyes, and takes a breath into her belly so that her voice comes out in a deep, powerful burst: "Oh, no you don't! I'm a prophet! I have the ear of God!"

The elders back away. Peeping from behind one another, they answer, "You have the ear of God? Good for you. We have the pen."

"God will punish you for writing down something different, for diverging from words that come to you through me, his prophet."

"The punished one predicts our punishment! Even if we suffer for it we will do it anyway, for the good of the community, for the peace of the community, for the honor of the community. Besides, personally it makes us feel better."

"It makes you feel better to deny me what is mine?"

They nod their heads.

"But why? How can this happen?"

"Too long a story. Also too late. You heard about Grimm's Law? All across the whole continent the sound of P, for instance, changed to F. Then G to K, T to D! Nobody could stop it! And The Great Vowel Shift, Miriam! Ah to Aiye. Ee to Eye. Think of it! So once upon a time maybe—we're not saying it's true, but maybe—women were prophets, angels, who knows what else? Powerful types. Then it happened. The Great Gender Shift! For you also a grim law. Whatever women did was changed to men did it. Miriam, you can't give us the Ten Commandments. Maybe you did give them, but the way we have to write it down it's Moses."

"I gave Moses life! I came first!"

"You know how it is with the younger child. God favors him."

"You say it. I haven't heard it from God."

"Trust us."

"I'll be a thorn in your side. I won't go quietly!"

"God doesn't like complainers. God doesn't like disobedient daughters. God doesn't like sisters who go out on their own."

"It was I who invented the cradle on the Nile! I who led Pharaoh's daughter into my scheme, I who brought the child's own mother to nurse. I—I—I . . .!"

"Miriam, you're beginning to stutter, like Moses. Don't think you can put yourself in Moses' place that way."

Miriam hides as the elders approach, knowing in advance what they'll say.

ON THE FOURTH DAY, Zipporah, Moses' wife, stands before her. She is beautiful, black as desert night, and speaks in her customary blunt way.

"You scorned me as your brother's wife, Miriam, but I scorn petty gloating. I want to know. Was it jealousy that goaded you?"

Miriam looks up wearily. "I, jealous? Of what?"

"On the way to Egypt from Midian, where God threatened Moses with death, I cut the foreskin from our son and flung it at the feet of my husband, who would otherwise have died on the spot, the commandment unfulfilled. You saved Moses the child, I saved the grown man. I gather you didn't like that! Still, I came to know how you are faring here. Not well, I see."

Miriam shields her eyes. "How should I fare?"

Zipporah is tall, her carriage superb, like those women of Ethiopia who, through secrets known only to their spines, walk with burdens on their heads and never tire. Though Miriam's gaze is hidden, Zipporah's burns. "Your punishment thrust you out of the camp, broke your power, snatched prophecy from you. It's true—how should you fare?"

"What was my crime?" Miriam at last tears her hand from her eyes. "I railed against you not because you saved my brother's life! You turned his head with lust! How else could he forget to circumcise a son? And you yourself complained he would not sleep with you when he received God's word!"

"If your wits were not so throttled by your banishment here, you'd see that meant he was drunk with God, not me."

"But you complained of it! You hoped to usurp Moses' passion for God into passion for yourself! And Moses, to fend you off, had to tear himself entirely from you! 'Have nothing to do with a woman,' Moses told us, awaiting revelation at Sinai, as if we consisted only of men! You are the cause of such misjudgment."

"Look around you, Miriam. You're banished here and I am free. God, it seems, is on the side of men's passion for women."

Again Miriam shields her eyes from Zipporah's stare. "The mystery of it gnaws at me nightly. Was it the very ferocity of your passion for Moses that gave you the courage to face the darkest aspect of God on that journey to Egypt? If so, I am punished for not seeing it! And for presuming into the heart of mystery beyond me."

"This is a new humility for you, Miriam!"

"We are flung back—prophets and ordinary folk—again and again. We struggle, flail, aspire with all our might, but the moment comes. No one knows when. The whirlwind sucks us in and spews us out again!"

"I am no prophet, Miriam, your family lays all claim to that. Yet I must say that's far from my reading of life. You should eat, drink, sleep with your husband, give birth to sons—live life! Your spirits have sunk too low."

"I am ground to dust."

"Then I'm sorry for you, in spite of . . .! If I have anything to say, Moses will never presume on prophecy as you did. Heaven forbid he should bring punishment like yours on himself!"

Miriam has already foreseen that such a moment will come for Moses, too, but again she shields her eyes and says nothing more.

ON THE FIFTH DAY comes Miriam's husband, Caleb. He offers to lie with her, to comfort them both. This is, of course, forbidden, but Caleb is a clear-seeing man, one of the messengers who will enter Canaan and report to the weary band of refugees that the promised land appears not threatening, but promising.

He has noticed that some of the proscriptions against women are neither provable nor practical. Such as the belief that women die in childbirth if they fail to light Shabbat candles, or that if a woman's stomach bloats after she drinks the bitter waters, she is proven adulterous. He has seen a servant drink the liquid by mistake, mixed with wine, and *his* stomach bloated. So would *all* stomachs bloat, including those of the administering priests. A whole tent full of ballooning bellies could not equal a shekel's proof of sexual impropriety.

A belly ballooned with sickness is a mockery of true fecundity. Maybe, Caleb says, they might restore a better and more natural order of things this very night. Then Miriam, who has been childless till now, like her powerful ancestors, Sarah and Rebekah (Caleb kindly adds), might conceive a child.

Despite their bravery, they are both too nervous for this to happen.

"Why is it," Miriam asks bitterly, "that your directness and honesty earn you honor in the world, while mine earn me nothing but scorn?"

Caleb is too good a husband to answer that. He merely murmurs soothing, loving things, and hints that though he is no prophet, he feels in his bones that such things will change before long.

ON THE SIXTH DAY, the women of the community come, urging Miriam to give up assaults on power, or at least to seek power couched in feminine wiles and apparent submissiveness.

"Don't you know you catch more flies with honey than vinegar, Miriam? And all men are flies!"

"Go away," Miriam answers. "Things have gone too far for that now. I want the same right to speak out as my husband Caleb and my brother Moses, to say what I think, and act on it."

"Poor Miriam," the women sigh. "She hasn't a clue."

Then they leave her.

ON THE SEVENTH DAY, Miriam prays to God, soundlessly, moving only her lips, as Hannah did, and on that day God is her visitor.

"They have written me down, O, My Maker, as a joke, a pushy woman who has to boss everybody, and have opinions, and get her own way. You are my witness that I strove to listen with all my soul and to speak bravely."

"Am I to blame if men distort my words? Am I responsible if outlandish tales are planted among my truths? Woman from Adam's rib, to begin with! Why would I do such a thing, when my good earth is there for creating? I molded man, I molded woman. Or it might be the other way 'round, I've forgotten. How can it matter? Since all my creation is good. But your scribes—oh, what appetite for revisionism! Whole committees for Hearsay Holy Writ!"

Miriam reminds God that when it was time for the Hebrews to start on their exodus from Egypt it was she who remembered Bitiah, Pharaoh's daughter. Miriam soothed her grief at losing Moses, wept with her at the destruction of Egypt's first-born.

"Loss! Death! Diminishment!" Bitiah cried out. "How have I deserved this?" Miriam wept with her at the loss of life on both sides, at the mother-loss of Bitiah. Because of

Miriam's tears, God had promised that she would have honor. That God would make her, Miriam, a prophet, a singer at the Red Sea!

"Now I who was promised reward am disgraced. How am I to understand our love for one another in all this confusion and suffering," Miriam pleads. "Am I beloved, or rejected? Am I cherished, or forgotten? This lifting up and hurling down of my spirit will kill me!"

God remains silent on the subject of Miriam's suffering, and instead spends the day teaching her various readings of God's own nature. God supplies Miriam with several views of the Deity, and brings up the subject of alternative readings of Bible narrative and law—midrash—those tolerant, sometimes baffling, wide-minded ways of saying, "Set these opposing opinions down beside one another. These and these are both the words of the living God."

Miriam protests that talmudic discussions are all very well, but she is disgraced before the people! How can she face them again? Better if she never emerged from banishment!

"Everything evil will be remembered and held against me," she says. "Leprosy, shame, punishment, expulsion."

"No," says God. "It won't be that way. You'll see. Go out."

"I look terrible," Miriam weeps.

"Not to me," says God. "Go out."

And when she comes out, all the people of the camp assemble and stand to greet her. They bow in reverence before her shining face, radiant with the beauty of the new-skinned. The people whisper that the shining of Miriam's face resembles the shining of Moses' face whenever he speaks with God.

(Millennia later, women would attempt to achieve such change in their appearance by visiting desert spas where skin is exfoliated and bowels are purged; where they rig you to a regimen of pushups and jogs and hi-lo-impact aerobics; where they serve meals of three spaghetti strands and one asparagus tip artfully arranged on a plate beside hot water to drink with a little lemon, so that the pounds drip off like sweat from a toiler on the pyramids, and where they send you out, a sparkling specimen, looking like the woman you were meant to be. But these women don't have in their faces what Miriam had in hers, when Miriam emerged from her seven days outside the camp, because their banishment to the desert is only a journey to a spa, while Miriam's was a journey inside herself to find there her parents, her husband, her kin, her neighbors, and whatever words she could locate for addressing God.)

Then the towering pillar of cloud began to move before them again, the waters of Miriam's Well bubbled up beside them once more and spilled over into a delightful stream that ran alongside their steps.

And then—did Miriam lead them along the way? Or did the combined weight of sorrow, joy, rejection, and exaltation crack her heart at last, so that she died?

Both, say the old legends, and ours must say the same. She both died and she persisted. She was ground down and she continued. She gave up and she endured.

Now and then, in the midst of such tearing oppositions, some spirit or energy entered her and she burst out in a song of joy and hope. Suffering and singing, she was like us. Miriam the daughter, the sister, the mother, the warrior, the wife, the prophet.

TAMAR

GENESIS 38:6–19

Judah got a wife for Er his first-born; her name was Tamar. But Er, Judah's first-born, was displeasing to the Lord, and the Lord took his life. Then Judah said to Onan, "Join with your brother's wife and do your duty by her as a brother-in-law, and provide offspring for your brother. But Onan, knowing that the seed would not count as his, let it go to waste whenever he joined with his brother's wife, so as not to provide offspring for his brother. What he did was displeasing to the Lord, and He took his life also. Then Judah said to his daughter-in-law Tamar, "Stay as a widow in your father's house until my son Shelah grows up"—for he thought, "He too might die like his brothers." So Tamar went to live in her father's house.

A long time afterward, Shua's daughter, the wife of Judah, died. When his period of mourning was over, Judah went up to Timnah to his sheepshearers, together with his friend Hirah the Adullamite. And Tamar was told, "Your father-in-law is coming up to Timnah for the sheepshearing." So she took off her widow's garb, covered her face with a veil, and, wrapping herself up, sat down at the entrance to Enaim, which is on the road to Timnah; for she saw that Shelah was grown up, yet she had not been given to him as wife. When Judah saw her, he took her for a harlot; for she had covered her face. So he turned aside to her by the road and said, "Here, let me sleep with you"—for he did not know that she was his daughter-in-law. "What," she asked, "will you pay for sleeping with me?" He replied, "I will send a kid from my flock." But she said, "You must leave a pledge until you have sent it." And he said, "What pledge shall I give you?" She replied, "Your seal and cord, and the staff which you carry." So he gave them to her and slept with her, and she conceived by him. Then she went on her way. She took off her veil and again put on her widow's garb.

COMMENTARY

No newly invented story could possibly compete with the dazzle of the biblical tale of Tamar, who, in a time of legal and social constriction of women, acts with the verve, daring, and sweep of a samurai.

Finding herself a childless widow, she dresses as a prostitute, sits at the crossroads, and lures her father-in-law to intercourse so she can conceive a child. This is the child denied to her first by his sons who one after another died following marriage to her, then by Judah himself, who in fear withholds his last son, Shelah, from the obligatory levirate marriage that would give Tamar progeny.

In my own midrash story, I have moved Tamar's command of choice even further. "Too young," is Judah's excuse for not giving Shelah as husband to Tamar. But traditional midrash tells a truer reason. Judah feared that Tamar brought disaster on his sons—two had already married her and died. One, Onan, bequeaths a name—onanism—to the masturbator who spills his seed. The other is Er, whose trespass is not named, though we are probably right in suspecting that he, too, must have sinned by enjoying sex without procreation.

In my story Shelah becomes Tamar's lover and he, not Judah, is the father of her child.

Tamar might have grown full with Shelah's child, and they might then have come forward to tell Judah: "See—the curse on your sons is removed! Shelah lives!" Then there would have been no need of crossroads or of prostitution. But that would have been to lose the first act of daring, seducing the father-in-law, in order to gain the second, seducing the son.

Besides, Judah's old jealous nature, honed years before in younger brother Joseph's company, might spring out again to wreak vengeance on the disobedient young couple. Judah's own taboo-transgressing intercourse with his daughter-in-law, though unwitting, is a necessary hubris-humbling event. Sin crouches at your door when least expected.

Childless women of the Bible generally count on God as womb-opener. Sarah. Rebekah. Hannah. Rachel. But Tamar does not pray for a child as Hannah does. Or weep or rail and despair as Rachel does. Or resign herself as Sarah does.

Tamar imagines and invents. She studies the characters of those around her, assumes a character for herself, chooses a setting, devises a plot, and brings it to its completion in dramatic confrontation. In short, she's the performance artist and dramatist of a novel she has written.

In my midrash, Tamar the novelist creates a double plot. The biblical entrapping of Judah for purely reproductive reasons is in my version intertwined with the love story of Tamar and Shelah. As the nurse muses at the end, he is the true and desirable progenitor of David, handsome and healthy as the King himself will one day be.

The character of Judah, who in the Bible version is portrayed as magnanimously forgiving of Tamar at the close of their episode, is in my version somewhat less lustrous. Judah's gracious condescension is brought into question. He is not the hero he appears in his own eyes. The young lovers have outsmarted him, and this is as it should be. His pardoning Tamar is the charity of one who possesses all the rights. Tamar enjoys no rights at all, save those to her wits. Until she bursts free of her bonds, she is imprisoned by patriarchal refusal: She cannot marry Judah's youngest son and she cannot marry anyone else, either—she is obligated to remain within Judah's family in her pariah situation of childless widow. Wit, youth, and courage toss charity back into the embarrassed lap of the condescender, and ingenuity inherits at the end.

Elsewhere, traditional midrashic rabbis are ready to heap anathema on the sexual behavior of women—on their tendency (ever since Eve) to lure men to impious behavior, and on their eagerness to resort to deceit.

In responding to Tamar's story, they are paradoxically ready to overlook everything: her adulterous behavior, her disguise as a harlot, and the snare she sets for Judah. She is instead praised for her modesty (the harlot disguise included a veil, *Genesis Rabba* reminds us), for not publicly shaming Judah over the pledges but instead quietly showing them to him (*ruah hakodesh,* the power of prophecy, had told her all would be well), and for her pious wish to have a child.

The contemporary reader will probably want, as I do, to emphasize the sheer breathtaking, custom-flouting effrontery of Tamar's behavior—deception, sexual seduction, harlotry, and patriarchal insubordination. All the better to set her courage and wit into highest relief. One wants to hear the swish of the samurai's sword as it cuts down clean, through barriers of reasons, excuses, and prohibitions against women, constricting lives as painfully as the bound feet of Chinese girls.

One question remained to be asked of the Tamar story: Why, being assured enough to steal seed, could Tamar not go further and capture rapture?

"Tamar: The Widow's Wager," provides the opportunity.

Tamar: The Widow's Wager

Men pass and whisper: "Tamar!" "Look out!" "Husband-killer!" They tell their sons: "Don't start with that one!"

They say no one knows how, exactly. Couch corruptions. Lively in bed is one thing, but this went too far! Woke in the morning and the man was cold. No warming with a kiss and a cuddle. Stone-cold! Not once but twice!

Tamar in her tent hears the whispers. No one comes near but her old nurse, who sees her agony and tries mirroring therapy: "How painful this is for you, my darling." And empathy therapy: "How I feel your suffering, my dove!"

"Stop that," says Tamar. "I'm thinking."

"Don't, my dove, my precious. Mourning and grieving are best for you now."

"I've no time," says Tamar. "Do you know how late it is? I don't need morning. I need evening. And bed. With a man in it who's not too selfish or feeble to father."

The nurse weeps. It's all too tragic. "No one dares come to your bed, my darling. A little denial might lift your spirit, but you can't lose your sense of reality altogether!"

"Go away," says Tamar. "It's not denial or reality I need now. It's something different!"

"What? What could that be, my darling? Different is always dangerous!"

"I won't know until I think of it. Go away and let me think."

Silently, secretly, in the night, Tamar sends for Shelah, Judah's youngest son.

"I wanted to see for myself anyway," says Shelah. "Is it true, what people say, you killed my brothers? Why would you do that—make yourself widowed and childless? There's no sense to it!"

Tamar is silent, only rocks back and forth, holding herself at her empty middle.

"I'm supposed to be your husband," says Shelah. "Would you kill me too?"

Not looking at him. Only her silent rocking.

"My brother Er died three days after marriage. Onan within the first week. Show me your face. Let me see the monster who kills. The one my father warned me of."

Slowly, Tamar lifts her veil.

"You're beautiful! Did my brothers want to keep you unmarred by childbearing? Was that their sin? I feel no fear. When can we marry?"

"Your father says you're a child. Go away."

"He says that only because he thinks you'll kill me, too. I don't think you will. Do you think my father will give you to me for a wife if I ask him?"

"No. He will say again that you're a child."

Shelah crawls into her lap where she sits on the floor. "Then I'll be your child, now that my mother is dead." Tamar enfolds him in her arms. They rock back and forth together. After a little, Shelah says, "You see? I am not too young to be your husband. Let me begin now."

"You have the sweetness of a boy, the ardor of a man," answers Tamar. "Your skin is silk. Your thighs are cedar trunks, your limbs are willow trees. One minute you nestle at my breast like a child, the next you want to plunge like a lion! Ah, I see how Judah saved the best for last! From this embrace there will be no turning back!"

Weeks pass. And when the old nurse comes to care for Tamar she asks in alarm, "Where are the cloths I must wash for you at this time of the moon? What—none? Death! Death! Who will help us?"

Tamar answers, "Calm yourself, dear Nurse. I was meant to have a child by Shelah, and now it is fulfilled."

"He is forbidden to you! Poor child, death is your portion. Judah will not let you go unpunished. What if Shelah should die like his brothers?"

"It is done, and Shelah has not died for it. Judah can rejoice!"

"Done, then, but not in the right way. Not with acknowledgments to power. This disobedience is death!"

"Judah sold his brother into slavery, betrayed his father's heart, and was forgiven!"

"Death! Death! My poor child. Don't compare yourself! Shelah is denied to you!"

"Then I will ensnare him," says Tamar with conviction.

"The son who was promised to you and then withheld? That is bold, I see the justice of your wish, but still . . ."

"No, not the son. But he is close to the son. A near relative. Be calm," says Tamar.

"My breath grows short! Blood pounds in my ears! I am too old for riddles! Speak plainly! Nothing could be worse than the terrors I am dreaming now!" The nurse tears at her hair. "You are beyond my help!"

"Not at all. There's much to do. First, fetch me the scented oil, and the paint pots. Loosen my hair. Ring my neck with ornaments. Put bells on my feet. Tie round my hips a girdle with bright bits of glass sewn in, with embroidered animals, open-mouthed and up-rearing. . . ."

"This brings death! What you are doing? Death!"

"Slide copper bracelets along my arms till they bite into flesh. Hang turquoise and mother-of-pearl at my forehead, and ring my eyes with sparkling black! Paint my lips crimson. Carry my belongings to the crossroads of Timnah and Enaim. Hang a scarlet curtain before my tent."

"Stop! Stop! I am your nurse, not your procurer!"

"Poor soul, you needn't be. Do the opposite! Keep men away from me."

"Ah, that's good news! But then why, my dove, sit there at all at the crossroads?"

"Only one will you allow to enter. Unless you procure him for me you cannot nurse me now."

"Woe is me! Say none at all, my pigeon. One is too many!"

"One. And it must be that one. Whisper his name in your brain. He deceived his father with a blood-stained coat. And his father deceived *his* father with goatskin-covered arms. So with false coverings I will deceive him!"

"I am faint! My heart won't stand this!" cries the nurse.

"My heart yearns to do God's will. As Judah was restored to righteousness, so may God reward my efforts, too."

The nurse weeps bitterly. "My poor widowed child, such daring in women draws death!"

At night, Tamar and her old nurse travel in disguise to the crossroads. Tamar seats herself at her tent, arrayed as a prostitute. Soon a man approaches, and Tamar calls out to him.

"Wise old man, can you tell me—if God strikes a man dead, should the nearest woman be blamed?"

"No need for such fears," answers Judah. "I am old but healthy."

"Or if a woman is left widowed and childless, should relatives intervene?"

"Naturally," says Judah, "they give her another son as husband. This they do for the sake of the deceased husband."

"Then is it better to wait for justice from God, or to wrest it one's self from life?"

Judah has by now entered Tamar's tent. "I've no wish to be rude," he says, "but I'm a busy man. Riddles are pastime for some, but I'm not Solomon, and you, if you'll pardon me, are no Queen of Sheba. Can we get on with this business?"

"Then as part of this business," Tamar says, "I will accept nothing from you now but pledges. Give me three—your staff, mantle, and cord."

"I wish all women would strike as fair a trade as you," says Judah.

He gives her the pledges, planning to redeem them next day, but as all the world knows, the prostitute who sat at the crossroads that night could not be found again. And though well satisfied with the night's transaction, Judah was uneasy at the thought of the pledges unredeemed, the payment not made to the prostitute whom no one knew.

As for Tamar, she exults. Judah has fallen into her snare. But the trickiest part is still to come. There is Shelah, who has his pride, his passion, his sense of male privilege. If the plot is to succeed, there can be no concealing from him the facts of the disguise, the crossroads, the lying with Judah his father. Soon scandal will break out—the pregnancy will show forth. Mercy, understanding, imagination must also show themselves if life is to continue. Tamar, the daring, dares once more and tells Shelah what she has done.

"Don't be jealous, my love. Judah's feeble manhood was soon spent. Not lavished on me, either, but dribbled off to one side as soon as he lay beside me. Between you and me, he's no Abraham. Sometimes an old man is just an old man. Then again—like father like sons, I suppose."

"Like me, you mean?" Shelah demands.

"No, no, not like you, my lion, my love!"

And so the drama unfolds. Word comes to Judah: "Your daughter-in-law has played the harlot!" Burn her! says Judah. Then Tamar produces the pledges, and Judah understands at once—it is a miracle of understanding! Because he withheld his last son from her, she was forced by harlotry to lay claim to her entitlement of a child. "She is more righteous than I," Judah says.

But again, there is Shelah. He too wants to claim his entitlement! How to keep Judah the lion from raging at the truth?

"Father," says Shelah, "I am eager to be the redeemer of my dead brother's life, and to raise up a child in his name by marriage to the widow, Tamar."

"But my poor boy," says Judah, "haven't you noticed that she's already conceived? She won't be left childless, nor your brothers without heir. And you know the whole unfortunate story—the night I stumbled upon her, disguised as a harlot. This woman has now been known by your two brothers and by me. That can't be very enticing for you."

"Out of respect I won't speak of your role here, Father. But I must say the thought of my dead brothers there before me binds me to her with curious strength, and with deep family loyalty.

"Well, family's family, after all is said and done. And since my child's already in her, I suppose there's no danger for you, which I had feared all along. And you mustn't let the thought that I was there before you spoil your pleasure.

"No, Father."

"I believed she was a prostitute. I was disgusted by the act, of course, I was thinking of your dear dead mother all the while. I was in and out before you could say a quick Kaddish. It's not as if there was lovemaking going on."

"I know that!"

"Nothing to be jealous of," says Judah.

"I'm convinced of it," answers Shelah.

"I didn't recognize her then and I probably wouldn't now. I barely look at women anyway."

"Don't be anxious on account of your character, Father. It's well known that you offered your own life for your brother Benjamin when Joseph held him hostage in Egypt. You're a good man."

"These things are complicated," says Judah with a sigh. "But I don't want you to feel cheated. Tamar's first-born will of course be a special child. But you can count on other children from her."

"I'm prepared to accept what God sends us."

Tamar watches the sparring of the father and the son. She sees that Judah is warm with sympathy for his son, who accepts uncomplainingly what Judah believes is the prospect of second-hand fatherhood.

"These women are to be pitied, you know. Their biological clocks are ticking away," says Judah, hiding from himself the winding down of his own biological clock. "Men don't have that problem. But now she's freshened, she'll go on bearing for you."

"I know that, Father," replies the respectful youngest son.

"I don't want you to feel cheated," says the old father.

"I'll try not to," says the beaming bridegroom, while Tamar looks modestly down.

Tamar and her handsome young husband receive Judah's blessing. The nurse joyfully prepares Tamar for the marriage bed once more. After a painful time of terrified babbling, she has recovered her wits and is now given to prophetic visions. She sits on the ground and muses:

"There will one day be a king whose name is David, a lusty lad, a poet and a singer. He will try to dupe Uriah into believing himself the father of his wife's love-child. But it is David who will be father to that child of Bathsheba's! The child does not fare well, but I see a happier course for this one of Tamar's.

"Tamar contrived to have Judah think himself the father of the child she conceived with his son, Shelah, her rightful spouse. Is not my Tamar, by right of wit and passion, a queen?

"This young couple will provide a tent of joy for their child, who will be ancestor to David. Thanks to my ingenious Tamar, who chose not a decaying seed but a vibrant one to match her own, King David will one day be as handsome and agile a lover of women as any. Like David's fortunes, Tamar's will be prospered by God, who values a true celebrator of life when one now and then appears!"

As for Tamar, she inwardly exults: "Child and lover, I have them both! It might have meant my death. Instead I have my heart's desire and am neither cast out from society nor imprisoned in it! I have earned a path, narrow and dangerous, but mine to walk on!"

LOT'S DAUGHTERS

GENESIS 19:23–36

As the sun rose upon the earth and Lot entered Zoar, the Lord rained upon Sodom and Gomorrah sulfurous fire from the Lord out of heaven. He annihilated those cities and the entire Plain, and all the inhabitants of the cities and the vegetation of the ground. Lot's wife looked back, and she thereupon turned into a pillar of salt.

Next morning, Abraham hurried to the place where he had stood before the Lord, and, looking down toward Sodom and Gomorrah and all the land of the Plain, he saw the smoke of the land rising like the smoke of a kiln.

Thus it was that, when God destroyed the cities of the Plain and annihilated the cities where Lot dwelt, God was mindful of Abraham and removed Lot from the midst of the upheaval.

Lot went up from Zoar and settled in the hill country with his two daughters, for he was afraid to dwell in Zoar; and he and his two daughters lived in a cave. And the older one said to the younger, "Our father is old, and there is not a man on earth to consort with us in the way of all the world. Come, let us make our father drink wine, and let us lie with him, that we may maintain life through our father. That night they made their father drink wine, and the older one went in and lay with her father; he did not know when she lay down or when she rose. The next day the older one said to the younger, "See, I lay with Father last night; let us make him drink wine tonight also, and you go and lie with him, that we may maintain life through our father." That night also they made their father drink wine, and the younger one went and lay with him; he did not know when she lay down or when she rose.

Thus the two daughters of Lot came to be with child by their father.

COMMENTARY

After the destruction of Sodom and Gomorrah, Lot, in his distraction and terror, resembles the stripped and outcast King Lear. Lear flees to a heath, Lot to a desolate mountaintop.

Lear was cruelly thrust out of doors by his unloving daughters, Goneril and Regan. Lot had once thrust his own daughters out of doors to pacify the rapists of the city he lived in.

Now Lot is isolated with his daughters, who have fled the destruction with him. The daughters believe themselves to be the last human beings left on earth, and discuss with one another how to remedy the situation after Lear/Lot falls asleep.

Bible sons are always distinguished, one from another: Cain and Abel, Jacob and Esau. Even Haman's sons are named. Lot's daughters—mere daughters, women—are undifferentiated. I will differentiate the daughters here, call them Goneril and Cordelia.

Traditional rabbinic midrash is no more openly condemning of Lot's daughters than of Lot, in itself a welcome surprise. Of the daughters they concede (in *Genesis Rabba*) that their intention is to do right in having offspring, "though one of them disgraced her father and called her son Moab, which means 'by my father.' " The daughters were the progenitors of two nations. Those nations, Moab and Ammon, are to be shunned, though gently, since the first produced Ruth, the second, Naomi. As for Lot, once he separated himself from Abraham and went to wicked Sodom and Gomorrah, he probably fell into lust for his own daughters.

But of the biblical event central to the early part of the story—Lot's thrusting his daughters outdoors to appease the lustful townsmen in order to spare his male guests—traditional midrash has nothing to say. We are filled with indignation, but the rabbis are not. Rape had not yet been expressed as the crime we now see it is. The rape of one's daughter could not, in that biblical setting, compare in horror to the failure to provide hospitality and shelter for a guest.

The best that traditional midrash could come up with was, "Woe to the wicked and woe to his neighbor."

How did the daughters feel about their father and his subjecting them to rape, which would have been the case if the angelic guests had not intervened? Neither biblical text nor midrash allows space for their words or feelings on the matter.

In my midrash, "Daughter-Wives of Lot," I allow for both.

Daughter-Wives of Lot: All Glorious Is the King's Daughter Within (but that shouldn't stop you from thrusting her out-of-doors when necessary): A Children's Play

A scene of desolation—smoke, fire below; cries, groans in the distance; ear-splitting cracks as ancient trees and building-stones explode; a dreadful creaking as if great chains have burst apart.

Goneril and Cordelia, in singed rags, stand over the sleeping form of Lot, their father.

GONERIL (*to Cordelia*): Fine, then! That's how it will be! You have your view, I have mine. But the act's the same. If you like, teach your children that one of us acted in piety—that's you of course—and in humility—you again, Cordelia. The other in lechery, defiance, whatever you want to call it. For myself I'll teach my daughters not to be meat thrown to ravenous dogs!

CORDELIA (*to sleeping Lot*): Your weak old age, that I

should guard . . . ! Instead I'll strip you bare as fruit trees, devour figs of your flesh like a scourge. Father, I long to ask your blessing for my wedding night. How can I? No one will bless it. Shame and scandal are wrapped in it. We are tied in a hideous knot, you and I, our strands stuck together with slime.

GONERIL: Now your authority's gone from every part of you but this, that rears at me its upraised warning. If the world's to end, what use is morality? Salt-stick mother, stony father. Life's turned hard! I'll make it flower if I can.

CORDELIA: Will people say I acted in lust? Then my excuse I was the hope of future generations will not wash. All last-hour things are desperate. Someone commits suicide at the threshold of escape, thinking the border closed that day will not reopen. Next day it does and lets travelers through. But he lies in his lodgings, a suicide, and his precious manuscripts vanished with his life. Foolish Walter Benjamin! Couldn't you wait? Couldn't I? No. I see the world emptied of life, my father old. Suppose he dies tonight? Better to extract his last elixir, bottle it in my womb, and deliver a cure to the world. But what if the brew erupts in monsters?

GONERIL: Then at least alive!

CORDELIA: If ever again I feel our father's touch on my cheek, I'll know the other hand's at harvest elsewhere, and a secret heat will scorch us both. Is this what a good daughter does?

GONERIL: We are more than daughters now! We are transmitters of the last particles of life. I'd call us global engineers! (*Addresses the sleeping Lot*) Leanshanks, roll over!

Sleep on your stomach some other time to keep your spittle from leaking down your throat! Look up to heaven with your sleep-shut eyes.

If the world's to end I'll have a night of pleasure first. Your rod will comfort me. I see a way to make it yield, to droop, to grovel in the dust like any slave.

CORDELIA: I won't listen!

LOT (*turns and groans. In his stupor, feigned or real, he reaches out and fondles his daughters' breasts.*)

GONERIL (*angrily striking away his hand*): Up to old tricks! If this seems hideous to you, Cordelia, remember how at home this father thrust himself at night through our door and fell on our beds.

CORDELIA: Poor man—he was drunk and confused. And always afterward wept for it. I sometimes think I only dreamed it in sleep.

GONERIL: When will you wake up? He thrust his hands upon us! Yet did not prevent those same hands from thrusting us through his door to be raped by the men of Sodom! As we would have been, if angel-visitors had not intervened! Once he'd defiled us himself, he felt he had no need to protect us from men of the town! Open your eyes, Cordelia, sleepwalker!

CORDELIA: I never remember things in quite the way you do, Goneril.

GONERIL (*angrily*): You never remember anything the right way! You're a dedicated forgetter!

CORDELIA: As I have forgotten this very moment how to proceed! Which parts go where? Horror turns me limp, I can't move. I am a virgin . . .

GONERIL: Ha!

CORDELIA: . . . deflowering my father's purple blossom! Didn't God bless the sacrifice of a son? He may bless this sacrifice also.

GONERIL: No one is sacrificed here, Cordelia! And don't compare us with Noah's sons, either. They had no motive but idleness and lust. We want to save humanity. God who promised progeny to our people must not be made a liar! The comparison is with Abraham in Pharaoh's court, passing Sarah off as his sister to save his life.

CORDELIA: Yes, I like it better when you make us seem less wicked.

GONERIL: Wicked? You call *us* wicked? Think of all the thrusting out of women to placate men! That poor, nameless concubine left all night outside the door to be raped by the townsmen, and in the morning cut up by her gentleman friend into 12 pieces and sent, by way of message, mind you, to the tribes of Israel. Think of Dinah and Tamar who were raped and made pariahs, huddled out of sight. And those old men like David with their cold, bony fingers, their patriarchal pinches, their pious palm-sliding up and down your rump. They'll abishag you to death if you hold still for it.

CORDELIA: But Father, our Father!

GONERIL: Look! Did you see? His eyelids fluttered! Even now he prods us on. Cordelia! Do you understand at last?

CORDELIA: I've gone below to drown in darkness. If I stayed above in light we'd all be dead. Vanished without trace, like the cursed Sodomites who burned in brimstone.

GONERIL: When we asked, Father, why you rushed us from our home you had no words for us. "Mother, mother," we cried. Our mother turned her face in pity toward our lagging sisters, and was struck to salt. But you pressed mercilessly on. "Move, you women! Shut your mouths," you said, "and run!"

CORDELIA: Ah, Mother! Your salt pours burning on my wound!

(Time passes. Lot's daughters in the final stages of pregnancy. Only Goneril slowly goes about the task of serving her father his meal; Cordelia lies ill on a pallet of leaves and branches.)

GONERIL *(to the sleeping Cordelia)*: Now we must each envy the other's son still in the womb. Only one can bear the covenant. If you had not fallen ill, sister, I would be obliged to poison you!

LOT: Here come townspeople! Climbing the mountain to jeer at us. Two pregnant sisters and their father, the last man in the world!

TOWNSPEOPLE: Here are two women, see, they are prophets! They foretold a future with no one in it but themselves and their drunken father! Oh, prophecy! Two deaf creatures, trying to hear God's word! Two chimpanzees, trying to think! Two sisters, named Deaf and Dumb, here's a riddle! When is a father shared by children and parent? When is my husband my begetter? When is a woman sister to her own son?

(They throw stones at GONERIL, who cowers behind CORDELIA on her pallet. After a time, they depart.)

CORDELIA (*stirring from her bed*): I think my fever is gone. Don't cry, Goneril. We were brave. If we've lost God's favor it's because we could not read such murky signs. What mortal could in all that smoky despair? We've done our best.

GONERIL: What we did was not for our sakes.

CORDELIA: We did it for the children.

GONERIL: We were daring. Think how often that has been rewarded.

CORDELIA: Tamar lured her father-in-law to bed.

GONERIL: Rebekah tricked Isaac and her son Esau.

CORDELIA: Abraham offered his wife to another man.

GONERIL: Jacob deceived his father. Leah deceived Jacob.

CORDELIA: Yet we have not won God's approval.

GONERIL: We must live without it.

(*A couple of louts from the town straggle up the mountain to jeer at them, at which a thunderous voice is heard*):

GOD: Ignorant laughers! My word is clear—no mystery: Plant your seeds! Make your efforts! Do! Strive! Create! If your efforts come to nothing, what of it? You weren't there when I made the locust, and whatever else causes your crops to fail! Plant again! Renew your efforts! Create more! Never stop striving in the midst of failure! These are the elements laid down for human life, and the daughters of Lot are to my liking, though they fail at reading the world. Laugh at yourselves, you ignoramuses! Which one of you has read my world without error?

(*The louts cower in fear—"Who, us?"—and scramble out of sight.*)

CORDELIA: So God is on our side, after all! I'm really

grateful! Though it would have been nice if all the people of the town could have heard, not just these stragglers.

GONERIL: And improved our reputations.

CORDELIA: Justified our misinterpretations.

GONERIL: Gave us credit for ingenuity and responsibility.

CORDELIA: Allowed us to take our rightful place among the righteous.

GONERIL: As righteous as Abraham, preserving himself at Sarah's expense.

CORDELIA: As righteous as Jacob, who followed his mother's vision of true covenantal succession.

GONERIL: And deceived his father, his brother, and his uncle along the way.

CORDELIA: As righteous as our mother.

GONERIL: Who in her pity and confusion helped neither her daughters nor herself.

CORDELIA: As righteous as our father, who in lovingkindness begot us.

GONERIL: This is unbelievable! Cordelia! You're forgetting everything again! Now is no time for repressing! Labor pains are coming on!

CORDELIA: Be calm, dear sister. I'll midwife you and then you'll midwife me. Every moment must be lived, evil and good alike. For look how intertwined they are—from our despised offspring of Moabite and Ammonite will come Ruth and Naomi, who will live honored lives, remembered for lovingkindness and redemption.

(*The sisters lie down in childbirth. From behind a tree, somebody throws garbage at them.*)

Daughters, Wives, Warriors

DEBORAH

JUDGES 4:4–10

Deborah, wife of Lappidoth, was a prophetess; she led Israel at that time. She used to sit under the Palm of Deborah, between Ramah and Bethel in the hill country of Ephraim, and the Israelites would come to her for decisions.

She summoned Barak son of Abinoam, of Kedesh in Naphtali, and said to him, "The Lord, the God of Israel, has commanded: Go, march up to Mount Tabor, and take with you ten thousand men of Naphtali and Zebulun. And I will draw Sisera, Jabin's army commander, with his chariots and his troops, toward you up to the Wadi Kishon; and I will deliver him into your hands." But Barak said to her, "If you will go with me, I will go; if not, I will not go." "Very well, I will go with you," she answered. "However, there will be no glory for you in the course you are taking, for then the Lord will deliver Sisera into the hands of a woman." So Deborah went with Barak to Kedesh. Barak then mustered Zebulun and Naphtali at Kedesh; ten thousand marched up after him; and Deborah also went up with him.

COMMENTARY

Of all women in the Bible, Deborah seems least in need of new midrash. Her text is heroic from first to last: she is prophet, judge, general, and she sings her own victory song.

She appears to have been dropped into the text from a very great height. She exists not for marriage or childbirth, belongs to no family narrative. Traditional midrash questions very little about her and has little to impart. But what is there is enough to suggest a drama of struggle within the Bible story of triumph. Deborah, says midrash, made mistakes. Instead of going to Barak, her husband, she made him come to her, a sign of disrespect. The midrashists conclude that "eminence is not for women" (Megillah, 146). They attribute to God the defense of their own marital vulnerability, adding wishfully that Deborah was punished by loss of prophetic power while she composed the song that speaks too much of herself.

On their midrash I have built my own: "Deborah: A Prophet of Air."

Deborah: A Prophet of Air

In the country of Ephraim, between Ramah and Bethel, lived a couple named Deborah and Michael, in the candle business. Deborah made the wicks and dipped the wax, and her husband carried the candles to the synagogue. Her name meant Little Bee, and she was so busy morning and night that people said it was the right name for her. To her husband, Michael, they gave nicknames—Barak, or shining face (from dipping his nose in the candle business), and Lapidoth, keeper of the flames, which made him feel powerful. Like Tony the Torch.

They kept the sanctuary lit up, but aside from that they were an ordinary couple, getting along, making a living. Then people discovered that for some reason the candles Deborah made burned longer in the sanctuary than any others. Word got around that Deborah had special powers. People began to say she was a prophetess. They came to her for opinions, and they called her a judge. Pretty soon she had to give up her duties in the candle business. She sat outdoors under a palm tree so that men, forbidden to sit with women in enclosed places, could ask for her judgments.

Deborah had her own career now, and Barak's business prospered. Everyone wanted to buy candles from the company founded by a prophetess and a judge. But everyone could see that as good as Deborah's new profession was for business, that's how bad it was for the marriage.

To make matters worse, Barak was a complainer. Nobody needed his complaints. People saw for themselves that this was a bad situation. How could a woman with so much power give her husband his due in respect? In fact, they said, she didn't. And her husband, the complainer, agreed. So life was difficult for both of them.

Deborah heard God's voice and was ready to do God's bidding. But first she had to stop and ask herself, "How will this look? How will Barak react? How will he feel about it? What will people say to his face? What will they say behind my back?"

So she was always anxious when she sat outdoors under a palm tree and judged, and Barak the complainer sat nearby and complained.

Deborah could hear him, just like everybody else. This is what he said.

BARAK: It's not right, not fair. It's humiliating and looks bad. My father wants to know why I stand for it. My mother and sisters ask why I don't make her pregnant.

"She's a prophetess!" I yell at them. "Can't you get that through your heads? My wife's a prophetess and a judge, and you don't just whistle when you want her, that's how it is!"

All day and into the night she sits outside under a palm tree, won't come into the house, won't look after things inside. That tree is where the nurse of Jacob's wife, also a

Deborah, is buried. If only my Deborah were that other Deborah! Not that I wish her dead—God forbid!—but as lowly as that nurse, as attentive to those she was meant to serve, as gentle and slow and submissive. In short, a good wifely servant!

I want to ask my wife, "Where are the receipts for that last shipment of candles to the synagogue?"

I can't send for her; she won't come. Too busy. Too exalted. Too proud.

I go to her. "Where is my linen tunic, that I meant to wear on the holy days? I can't find it. Nothing's where it should be!

Meanwhile, Deborah the prophetess was sitting under the palm tree, trying to attend to petitioners, trying to give out judgment, trying not to hear Barak, and also listening to her own thoughts.

DEBORAH: I never asked for this splendor, this poetry, these spasms of insight and language that tear my life! Potentates and poor folk come for judgment. Into the misery of human strife the voice of the judge strikes its sword, cuts and cauterizes like healing fire. "Slice the child in two," says Solomon. And the rivalrous mothers soon reveal the impostor. That's what I want to do! Burn through confusions of ordinary life! Make my mouth a cup for God's crystal clarity!

And Barak went on complaining.

BARAK: My wife gives me a serious, mournful stare. Considers my request as if I'm asking a talmudic riddle. If a man plants a tree in a corner of his land and the branches grow over the wall onto the neighbor's side, who owns the fruit? You know the kinds of things they think up! It's only my linen tunic. Why is she giving it so much thought? Why not just go home and find it for me? It's not as if I have so many tunics to my name. Having a prophetess and a judge for a wife didn't make us rich!

What is she thinking? That I should look for it myself? That she has more important things to do?

People line up to speak to her. No one seems to realize I'm still her husband, with husband's rights. I can hear remarks, grumbles from the crowd. They think I'm using up more time than I'm entitled to, taking advantage of our relationship.

One of the crowd even calls out to me in a rough voice, "Michael, finish already!" No one has called me Michael in years. My name's been Barak ever since I started my candle business for the synagogue. It's like a Guild insignia. Like wearing a seal with light on it. They called me that. "Peace be with you," they called out, "face lit with light!" Barak. Or, Lapidoth—Flames. "Have a good fast day, Flames!" Now all of a sudden it's Michael.

DEBORAH: A woman named Yael comes to where I sit and judge under the palm tree. She has no question for me, only homage. Many thanks, I say, now I must go on to those who need me. But she won't leave, she says, before telling how I inspired her to change her life, show courage, act on principal, love justice more than safety or domestic harmony, and remember that beyond husband and children lies the world.

That makes me sigh, of course. Young women catch idealism like a fever, they have no notion of the terrible cost of freedom, or even that it is never in the end what they think freedom might be, but only a tethering to another form of dedication.

She vows her loyalty like a young knight and swears to put her life in service of mine if need arises.

Thanks, thanks, I say, urging her with my eyes to leave, to notice how the crowd of petitioners has swelled, has started to hum with its impatience.

And Barak can still be heard by everyone.

BARAK: I'm supposed to be quiet. Modest. Hold myself back. *She's* a bee. That's her name. Buzzing all day outdoors, never quiet. Drone, drone, buzz, buzz!

"Where is my tunic?" Watch out, I'll get a judicial opinion! Buzz, buzz, drone, drone! "The tunic, which is of fine linen, may be equivalent in value to three ephahs of oil and two of barley, provided there is no spot thereon."

Oh, it's intolerable! Philosophy is no substitute for a tunic!

My wife is a prophetess and a judge! It's like being married to a caravan of desert-wanderers. Each of her limbs is packed with opinions. Her brain is filled with visions of the future. In that case, she should tell me what I'm going to wear tomorrow!

Not far from here lives a man named Boaz. A worthy person, but no worthier than I. Boaz married late in life. Took a poor widow named Ruth as his wife and lived happy ever after. He asks her for a thing and she produces it. She takes, not gives, orders! All day long she's busy carrying out the requests of her husband and her mother-in-law. Doesn't have a minute to think! What a happy life! There's no doubt Boaz will have a clean tunic come tomorrow.

As for me, I'll wear one of my wife's opinions around my shoulders.

"Oh, Barak," she says. "If only you listened with more patient care so that the voice of the Almighty might fill you full of deeper needs!"

Well, that's it exactly, there's the injustice! Why her, not me? Side by side for years in our candle business, I doing twice the work, doing everything she did, then trudging to the synagogue with all those lit candles—we put fire to them in the shop to make sure every one of them was a burner. We never padded bills, sold shoddy merchandise, or defaulted on a delivery date. So why? Why not me? Don't I have a million opinions about everything? Don't I see weird figures in the corners of the room, especially late at night when I can't sleep? That's when Deborah, my darling bee, used to be my comfort. Her little wings would fan my brow. "There, there, don't be afraid. I'm here. It was just a dream!"

Why did she talk me out of my visions? I could have been a prophet, too!

I can't help it if people hear me sobbing. I'm so unhappy. When are you coming home?

She's giving me that melancholy stare again. Oh, no, she's going to foretell my future, and it can't be good, I don't even have a clean tunic to wear.

All right, my wife is a prophetess and a judge—and all for the glory of Israel! But Israel isn't all glory! What about us little people? We go on eating and sleeping, getting undressed and dressed in the same tunic day after day! It isn't fair to say that only the large and glorious things in life—ideas and justice and battles and victories—are all that matter. What about home? What about the little everyday domestic things that mean so much to a man? What about my tunic?

DEBORAH: Petty matters of the day, covetous neighbors, the envious spouse, the improvident husband, the dissolute son—in the midst of these pathetic human entanglements, the Creator's voice speaks to me of deliverance for Israel from a tyrant who preys on wayfarers, robs and kills. For 20 years we had no means of warding off Sisera's might.

Now the voice of God speaks. "Up, Deborah. War against the tyrant. Take Barak your husband with you."

It is the same voice that cursed Eve with subservience to her husband's will, her husband's desire. Now we see that God reconsiders. That curses, too, may change to blessings. Grow, swell, advance!

BARAK: Ah, thank God, at last she's getting up! She's moving away from the detestable palm tree! A husband still exerts some power over his wife!

What? Battle? My wife, a prophetess and judge, is also now a general? Please, there's a limit. I warn you. If there's no tunic and no dinner again this week, I won't answer for our marriage. I can find a rabbi to give a *get* even to a general just as quick as to any household drudge who can't produce a son.

So where are you going? Where's the war? Funny, I don't see Boaz's wife going off to fight!

Oh, well, if it's only you and God who know about this war then it's all right, isn't it? We won't worry about being attacked, will we?

Oh, I see, well, thank you for making a place for me in your army! Ten thousand men under me is not bad, I'll admit. But undoubtedly the enemy general will have twenty thousand men. Sisera has been unopposed for 20 years. If you've heard news that things will be different this time, you'd better come with me, Little Bee. Then the two of us together can sting Sisera to death.

DEBORAH: Barak asks me to ride with him in battle against Sisera. For safety and courage. Then at the decisive moment he wants me to fall back, leaving him clear victor, his head the highest.

I am willing. Sisera must be killed. If Barak can do that, let it be done by him.

BARAK: Yes. Even if people will say that the victory isn't mine. That Sisera was delivered into the hands of a woman. Fine! They'll say it no matter what. That's what it's like to be married to a prophetess and a judge. And since I am, I think I ought to get a little protection out of it, if it's not too much trouble. So I don't go headlong to my death. Haven't I just been telling you? Glory is all very well, but a clean tunic can come as close to the inner meaning of life as a spear through the heart!

DEBORAH: But here are 900 iron chariots crashing down upon Israel and where is Barak? He waits for me.

Up, Barak! The Almighty marches before you!

And so Barak rises up and all of Sisera's men fall. But Sisera escapes! And if I pursue, our men will jeer that Sisera was delivered into the hands of Barak's wife.

When it seems that everything is lost, all our pains for nothing as the tyrant escapes, news comes that Sisera, fleeing, sought refuge (or was he lured there?) in Yael's tent. And she, that inspired warrior who claims me as inspiration, soothed him first with milk as if in mockery of mother-care and then, as he slept, aimed her blow!

Up, Barak, to Yael's tent! She has killed your enemy for you, driven a tent pin through his brain while he slept in her bed. Your enemy has been delivered into the hands of a woman, it was foretold. But God has spared you this shame—the woman is not your wife!

Up, Barak, and sing! "There was no deliverance until you arose, oh, Deborah, in Israel!" Up, Barak, sing a new song, a victory song. Your name is in it, and Yael's. But your wife is called Warrior and Deliverer. And you must learn this song, never heard before among our people. Up, my poor Barak! Here is a new song for husbands to sing.

BITIAH

EXODUS 2:5–10

The daughter of Pharaoh came down to bathe in the Nile, while her maidens walked along the Nile. She spied the basket among the reeds, and sent her slave girl to fetch it. When she opened it, she saw that it was a child, a boy crying. She took pity on it and said, "This must be a Hebrew child." Then his sister said to Pharaoh's daughter, "Shall I go and get you a Hebrew nurse to suckle the child for you?" And Pharaoh's daughter answered, "Yes." So the girl went and called the child's mother. And Pharaoh's daughter said to her, "Take this child and nurse it for me, and I will pay your wages." So the woman took the child and nursed it. When the child grew, she brought him to Pharaoh's daughter, who made him her son. She named him Moses, explaining, "I drew him out of the water."

COMMENTARY

Bitiah, Pharaoh's daughter, can be an endless source of fascinating speculation. She is mentioned in I Chronicles 4:18, included there with the descendants of the tribes, as if she were one of them. And maybe, by then, she is. The midrashic rabbis translate her name as Daughter of God, *bat-yah* ("The Holy One, blessed be He, said, 'Moses was not your son, yet you called him son. You are not my daughter, yet I will call you daughter' " *Leviticus Rabba*).

How did Bitiah defy Pharaoh her father? How did she slip the baby Moses past him? What did Pharaoh know? Like the daughters of tyrants in our own time—like Svetlana, Stalin's daughter—Bitiah might want to protest that her experience of her father was not that of a despot but of someone always playfully tender.

Midrash is silent on many of our questions about Bitiah. What it does tell us is that after Miriam's death, Caleb, her husband, married Bitiah (cited in Ginzberg's *The Legends of the Jews,* vol. vi). What a glorious imagining! It matches in humanity what the midrashists conjured up to bring Hagar's and Abraham's lives full circle: After Sarah died, Abraham married Keturah, who was in reality Hagar, the concubine who had been banished by Sarah. Here, once again, is the posthumous linkage of two women, both heroines of the Hebrews' exile in Egypt, Miriam and Bitiah, whose courage made possible the survival of the Hebrews.

Did Bitiah join Exodus? What happened to her on that glorious and terrible night of fire, smoke, and death, when the first-born of the Egyptians were destroyed and the Hebrews left their servitude and marched out to freedom under God's banner? Torn by the choice between loyalty to homeland or to her foster son, appalled by the destruction of her own people, did she go or stay? In my midrash, a journalist of the Jewish Press pursues answers, even in the jeweled burial place of a royal Egyptian princess, to bring us "Bitiah: Memoir of a Tyrant's Daughter."

Bitiah: Memoir of a Tyrant's Daughter (as interviewed in the Jewish Press)

(The scene is a royal Egyptian tomb. Pharaoh's daughter is upright in her sarcophagus; the lid has been opened for the interview. Her mummy wrappings are gorgeously decorated with gold ornaments. Likewise, she is surrounded by many beautiful earthenware objects in various states of disintegration, and gold figures of slaves and animals. J.P., the Jewish Press journalist, is seated on a low, three-legged stool, scribbling furiously on a pad on his knee. He has for the time being removed his yarmulke from his head and slipped it into his pocket, since he is not sure what the halakhah, *or even the* minhag, *would be about the wearing of yarmulkes in Egyptian tombs.)*

J.P.: Your Highness, Excellency. I'm not sure I have the correct title for you. If not I apologize. Have you any thoughts, especially at Passover, about the Exodus from Egypt? From your own or Egypt's point of view, so to say?

BITIAH: Call me Bitiah. I am considered a righteous Egyptian in your Talmud, and given a Hebrew name.

J.P.: Bitiah. Thanks for the informality. And now, can you . . .

BITIAH: Have you noted, by the way, the long association of Egypt with Jews? First, rescuing Joseph from his brothers, then Moses from death. We have been, you might say, the instrument of your salvation.

J.P.: We certainly speak at length about that in the *Hagaddah*. Not in so many words, of course, but I definitely get your drift. Now about your own view of the Exodus . . .

BITIAH: I have looked into your books. Your sages wrestle with the question of why your God, having put you in Egypt, where you shared in our incredible Nile-favored fertility, kept you there for 400 years. Naturally, things change. First you had good fortune, then not so good.

J.P.: Yes, in fact, we were slaves. However, then came the Exodus, and I wonder how you see . . .

BITIAH: They say that even in the very worst times, every Egyptian woman had her Jewish child, did you know that?

J.P.: No! Really? But I thought that you alone, in great secrecy, were the one who rescued . . .

BITIAH: No, no, my father knew. He was not the tyrant you media people like to portray. You have no idea how loving he was to me.

J.P.: This is fascinating. Then you feel that the whole story is simply a . . . but wait, do you mean that you were able, openly, to . . . ? That you were able to just . . . ?

BITIAH: What do you do if your father is *considered* to be a tyrant, your country *considered* to be a tyranny, and you are a woman? You can hardly go to battle. You save one child.

J.P.: Well, it gets a little complicated, doesn't it? You say your father knew. About your rescuing the Hebrew baby

Moses from the Nile—that's what we're talking about, isn't it? But then the whole thing about Pharaoh not letting the Hebrews go, and the hardening of his heart, and all that, do you mean that it . . . ?

BITIAH: We were chosen to be the land of your exile. We, Egypt, and not another. Pharaoh understood his role! Do you know the Mathew Arnold verse: "This world—so various, so beautiful and new"? There it is, the necessary jigsaw puzzle. No piece without its purpose. The whole, you might say, Calder mobile. Shapes and materials and tones, all assembled into balance. All in need of one another for their being, though they may not of course know that.

We, Egypt, were the variation into which you had to fall to renew yourselves. We are the instrument of your redemption.

J.P.: Okay, got that. And now I think our readers would love to know what he was like. Moses? As a child?

BITIAH: I am often asked that question. Handsome. Strong. Athletic. Thoughtful. Willful, too. I delighted in him. Had I conceived a child by a royal Egyptian he could not have been more like my father, Pharaoh, than Moses was!

J.P.: Then the story about Moses' stammer—is that something we should discount?

BITIAH: Ah, it was the one thing that marred his perfection! From the moment he could speak, he stammered. It became a torment to me. I hired tutors, and so on—all useless. You may have heard some story about the child's having put a coal to his lip? Or that Pharaoh my father set before this baby two dishes, one of gold and one of burning coal, to test whether his understanding was great enough to threaten

Pharaoh, and that God directed his hand to the coal? Nonsense! I would never have permitted it!

J.P.: Then how . . . ?

BITIAH: Is your stylus sharpened? Cross out those fancy little tales your rabbis liked to make up about the Torah. Here's how it happened. It was the way of my father, Pharaoh, to call the children of the household to him from time to time, and question each in turn to learn the nature of their minds. One day he came to Moses.

"Who is your mother, Moses?" my father, Pharaoh, asked. The darling pointed to me.

"And who is your father?"

Little Moses looked helplessly about him. The children began to giggle. My father, Pharaoh, tickled Moses on his legs, his chin, with his royal pennant whip, and poor little Moses began:

"M-m-my f-f-f-father . . . , m-m-m-my f-f-f-father . . . "

This went on for some minutes. I can tell you, I was in agony. Then Pharaoh my father released Moses with a playful flick of his pennant whip. But the damage was done. I wept, I punished, I withdrew my love and then restored it again. Whatever I tried was no help. Moses could never rid his tongue of its blight. Yet here, too, I have read that this very affliction became a mark of Moses' distinction! So we illustrate again—our Egyptian contribution.

J.P.: Believe me, we don't stop hearing about it for eight whole days and nights! But to get back—have you any memories of the actual event, I mean the Exodus itself, I'm sure our readers would love to . . .

BITIAH: On that last, terrible night—fires, smoke, screams—I encountered Moses' mother.

J.P.: No! Really? That *is* news! In fact it's a scoop! I think I can swear to it that no one's ever . . .

BITIAH: Yes, there she was, running here and there, terribly upset. I knew her by this time. Yokheved. A wet-nurse for my child, they told me when I fished him from the Nile. But I knew. It was all too conveniently staged. I wasn't a fool! First this young Miriam comes bursting out of nowhere and says, "Oh, you found a baby in the Nile! Isn't that amazing! Now you'll need someone to nurse it and I happen to know a woman who just gave birth, with enough milk pouring out of her breasts to feed an army! I went along with it. Why not? I don't mind if other people's plans work out for them if they suit my purpose as well. And I felt the need of a child of my own just then. Especially a handsome, healthy one like Moses. I'll tell you the truth—it was a sickening sight to see those little Hebrew baby corpses floating by. And then, suddenly, here was a lively one! It was as if it called out to me!

J.P.: Yes, well, we're all grateful to you for answering the call, of course, but you were saying about the mother. Did you, actually, *speak* to her?

BITIAH: "My brother," I said, "is the first-born of Pharaoh, and will die on this terrible night! Can you not save him as I saved your son?"

Her eyes streamed with tears. I think it was with pity, but it may have been all the smoke. She ran away to her hovel.

J.P.: Without answering?

BITIAH: Not a word. So I knew there was nothing to be done. Yet I ask you, wouldn't it have been appropriate if some Jew came forward to save an Egyptian as I had done to save a Jew? Oh, I know what you'll say. My father's decree that the Hebrews' first-born sons should be drowned was made by a man, Pharaoh. The other decree, that the first-born of the Egyptians should be killed, was of God. Yet Pharaoh had the power of a God!

J.P.: Yes, well, up to a point, I gather.

BITIAH: Those encounters between the Hebrew's God and my father-God, they are all written down. You and the readers of your newspaper read them every year. No need to rely on my word! The pages are filled with male rage and ram-headedness. It wasn't only Pharaoh whose heart was hardened!

J.P.: Oh, I see what you mean. Is this, would you say, a feminist approach you're taking?

BITIAH: It is the approach of common sense and understanding. Pharaoh and your Hebrew God were like gladiators in an arena. "Stand back," they said to the people, Egyptians and Hebrews alike, "or when I swing my mighty arm you'll be hit!"

When the plague of frogs came upon us, the magicians of Egypt didn't care about the suffering of the people. They showed they could create more frogs! More serpents! More water turned to blood!

J.P.: Yes, but let's be fair to your side! The record also shows that Pharaoh's heart was hardened. That means, really, against his will! What this does to the Jewish idea of free will we won't get into here, because it's just too . . .

BITIAH: Yes, Pharaoh let his people suffer through these plagues of blood, boils, lice, rats, darkness, and wouldn't give in. But what about the hard heart of the Hebrew God? Who made *that* happen? Couldn't God, through his mighty power, have shortened the contest so that the side he was going to help, the Hebrews, would be released at once? Weren't they still suffering, dying of starvation and exhaustion at their day-and-night brickmaking during the weeks of this contest of might! Did God forget that the purpose of the whole thing was to relieve the suffering of the Hebrews? Did Pharaoh forget he was the father of his own people? The mighty monarchs shut their ears to the groans around them, the sights and smells of rotting flesh that fell on Jew and Egyptian alike. The mighty ones battled on, adding horrors. And no distinction made by your God for Hebrews—they were wading in the same blood!—until the seventh plague! Gnats, I believe.

J.P.: Excuse me, are you saying there were atrocities on both sides?

BITIAH: I am asking if you think there is some reason why everything couldn't be settled at once, instead of dragging it on and on? Couldn't God have *softened* Pharaoh's heart?

J.P.: Maybe God felt it *should* take weeks or months or however long it took. That way, the world and the text would take notice, and the lesson be truly learned. I grant it was painful for your people! But maybe they had to have the power of God driven home to them, so to say. So people would follow a moral course in the future.

BITIAH: I beg your pardon, I don't like to harp on things

painful to *your* people. But just an eyeblink of time after that, who feared the power of your God? Hitler? His magicians of fire and smoke were greater than your God.

J.P.: Sorry, I'm no theologian. Elie Wiesel actually lived through all that. He believes God sat at the gates of Auschwitz and wept. Personally, I can't understand why God had to do that. Think of the power of God in Egypt! Was it because of free will? Did things go too far, till they were out of God's hands? Sometimes they are and sometimes they aren't—look at Egypt!

BITIAH: My father, Pharaoh, would never have sat at the gates of Auschwitz and wept! He would have destroyed the train tracks leading there!

J.P.: Yes, well, I just can't tell you how many books have been published on this very subject, it's a real debate. People say, "All right, if God couldn't, then at least Roosevelt should have done something. . . ."

BITIAH: And while we're on the subject, couldn't God have created us all to act mercifully?

J.P.: Well, there you are again, no getting away from it, same old question every time—how do you create humankind? Should human character be limited to the same good things and no development? Or do you put in everything, good and bad, and let the person choose—that's your free will right there—so there's chance for growth and development. Not to mention suspense and drama, because nobody knows what's going to happen, ever. Of course, as a journalist, there can never be too much suspense and drama for me! But when I'm with my wife and kids, I think,

"How could it hurt to be able to count on good things happening? At least not bad, God forbid!"

BITIAH: Pharaoh, my father, always knew what would happen. He gave commands and they were followed. At least until the encounter with God. That was the end of certainty for him. And I must say, a wonderful way of life was lost.

J.P.: For those in the Palace, you mean!

BITIAH: Naturally.

J.P.: But the story, the drama, the narrative pace! Think how dull life would be. No heroes! No victories! No transcendence! No goals! No Pesach!

BITIAH: You can't have it all ways, you know. If you like the way these male power figures handle things, setting up conflict and struggle, then you're going to have to put up with the opposite of those nice things you're so fond of. Defeat. Suffering. Tragedy. Why not think about something else for a change?

J.P.: For example, your devotion to Moses, your son . . .

BITIAH: . . . and my husband . . .

J.P.: I beg your pardon?

BITIAH: Moses my son and husband.

J.P.: But—oh, surely not . . . ?

BITIAH: Does the news come as a shock? No doubt you're more familiar with our Egyptian custom that allows brothers and sisters of the royal family to marry one another, for who else can fitly do so? Moses became my husband. We broke no blood taboo.

J.P.: True, you weren't Oedipus and Jocasta, but it takes some getting used to—Moses married to Pharaoh's daughter!

BITIAH: I am to Moses what Hagar is to Abraham, what the Queen of Sheba is to King Solomon, what Queen Cleopatra is to Antony! I am Egypt!

J.P. (*gazing raptly*): Ah!

BITIAH: Oh, your rabbis tried to tame me! They gave me a sweet Hebrew name, Bitiah. And I am Bitiah. But I am also Fatimah! Of the thousand dark, enticing movements!

(*Belly dance music plays. The mummy wrappings stir.*)

J.P. (*seized with panic*): Please Bat—Fit—imah! I appreciate all your . . . but don't, please . . . I wouldn't want anything to . . . !

(*Music subsides.*)

BITIAH: But then, of course, like Oedipus, Moses had his fatal flaw. Subject to rages, radical impatience. He had to flee Egypt! The story was put about by the Hebrews that Moses killed an Egyptian to save a slave from a beating, but did you know that the Egyptian he killed was a royal relative? With him out of the way, Moses would be nearer to Pharaoh's throne when my father died. Was this an act of Jewish loyalty or of Egyptian ambition?

J.P.: Under the circumstances, a difficult question!

BITIAH: And when Moses returned to Egypt, was it for the sake of the Hebrew slaves, or to spend his nights with me once more?

J.P. (*embarrassed*): Even more difficult. Both, maybe?

BITIAH: Those gladiatorial contests between Moses and Pharaoh to see who could create more snakes, frogs, gnats, blood, darkness—didn't you suspect all along they were fighting over a woman? I was their Helen!

J.P.: Like the Trojans and Greeks, you mean? But the

people—the Hebrew slaves who had to be freed! God heard their outcry! Read Exodus 6:5!

BITIAH (*coldly*): Are you implying that I have not read my husband's work?

J.P. (*in confusion*): No, not at all! I'm afraid that's just a reflex on my part. They say that all the time in yeshiva—read this, read that.

BITIAH: Yes, read this, read that. The indispensable five books of my husband's oeuvre! On which, believe it or not, I have never collected a penny of royalty. Never mind, I *am* royalty. In Exodus 6:5, God heard the outcry of the Hebrew slaves. And awarded them as spoils to the victor.

J.P.: And because Moses was the victor . . . ?

BITIAH: Yes.

J.P. (*laughing hard*): So Moses took all these people as his own slaves when he left! Forget liberation and freedom!

BITIAH (*sternly*): I am suggesting alternative readings here. You'd do well to broaden your habitual views a little. Think of the rules and burdens Moses imposed on them when they got out. Is a covenanted Jew, by any stretch of the imagination, liberated into freedom?

J.P. (*with some cunning*): And did Moses take his Helen along, too?

BITIAH: Ah, yes, there's the difference. Helen came from Greece to Troy. When Troy fell she left with the victors, her own Greek countrymen. I was of Egypt, a country devastated by war with Moses, and bereft of all firstborn sons.

(*She pauses, then says proudly*): Yes! I went with Moses!

J.P.: But—but—you're never mentioned again in Exodus!

BITIAH: Haven't we learned by now how much the tale is the teller's? I admit it was awkward, I kept a low profile. Moses had picked up another wife, Zipporah, before his return to Egypt, so there we were with two mothers on the journey through the wilderness, Yokheved and me, and two wives, and I counted in both categories! And Moses was an edgy man! It seemed best to steer clear on that 40-year journey. I understood we'd renew our marriage when we got to the Promised Land and were finished with all the irritations of moving. I kept my supply of salves, ointments, oils, perfumes, and preservatives. My youth and beauty lasted the trip. But Moses never made it, poor old man! He had one of his "Nobody-tells-me-what-to-do" fits again and hit a rock with no more thought than when he struck down the Egyptian he shouldn't have. Because of the impatience of Moses, God widowed me, and I was alone in a foreign land. Not among my own people, either. I was with Yokheved my mother-in-law and Miriam my sister-in-law.

J.P. (*slyly*): And like Ruth did you serve your mother-in-law?

BITIAH: Certainly not! I, too, was the mother of Moses!

J.P. (*sighing*): What else happened on the trip?

BITIAH: The seven days of Miriam. She was put outside the camp. Punished for criticizing her brother. Moses said God wanted it that way. We all idled about the camp, hung about in the stillness like a sidetracked train waiting for a new engine. Our engine was there all the while, in the column of cloud that swung between heaven and earth, hanging over our camp like smoke from the sidetracked train we resembled. I was irritated. Angry. And grieving for my country. One day I approached the column of cloud . . .

(Bitiah's voice trails off. The wall behind her floods with light. We see her shadow-figure enter the column of cloud, which at once transforms into a wind tunnel, spins her round and round, sucks her hundreds of feet into the air. Then the glare dims.)

J.P. (*breathless*): What happened there? Was that you? Did you actually see God? Feel God there? It looked so—violent!

BITIAH: Yes, all my questions shook out of me there. "Why so much torment? Horror? Punishment? Death? Why *you* for a God? Why not the gentle, generous Nile, which at least, when it drowns us, leaves us drenched in richness?" I was dropped to earth, which caught me in her bosom. Manna drenched my lips with sweetness. The air was fragrant, the light in the sky an exquisite blue. I wept with joy. More questions shook from me: "How have I deserved this bounty, beauty, kindness, love?"

Such was my encounter with God. What is yours?

J.P.: Oh, I don't go in for that. Follow the rules and keep my nose clean is more my thing.

BITIAH: How boring of you!

J.P. (*goaded into sneering*): So what are you saying, Bitiah? You became a prophet too, like Miriam?

BITIAH: Why would I do that? I'd had enough of seers, Egyptian and Hebrew! No—I took another Jewish husband. But that was after Miriam died, leaving Caleb to me. A nice symmetry, when you think of it. First Miriam provided me with a baby, then a new husband. Moses sent Caleb into

Canaan to spy out the land, you recall, and Caleb returned with a report of bounty at last. What the Hebrews had pined for since their exodus from Egypt, the land of plenty. "You long for Egypt's fleshpots," the Hebrews jeered at one another, as if eating were a sin. But the promise of food in the new land was always "milk and honey," as though Hebrews were meant to sip like hummingbirds. It was I, Pharaoh's daughter, Princess of the Nile, who was the reminder, the living bridge between the longed-for forbidden fertility of Egypt and what was piously translated to milk and honey in the new Jerusalem!

J.P.: But clearly your—forgive me—bones, Princess, are here in Egypt, and not there in the Promised Land!

BITIAH: Egypt reclaims its own. Journeys are not difficult for us. And death is our greatest journey. I had, as I've said, my supply of salves, ointments, oils, preservatives. Joseph's bones were carried out. Why not Bitiah's body carried in?

J.P. (*gallantly*): May I say, Bitiah, that your sarcophagal beauty is very great. And that your sense of the complex interdependence of all life is inspiring!

BITIAH: My sense of the interdependence of all life is, if *I* may say, born of the teeming Nile. I don't vaunt my own actions, mind you, but look at what I did. I made no speeches, declared no contest. I sent no minions to act for me. I reached into the water and drew out one Hebrew child. One. One saved one. An act from which meaning never ceases to flow, through ages and worlds.

(*The sarcophagus shuts. The interview is over. The Jewish Press journalist carefully picks his way past the strewn rubble of royalty.*)

ESTHER

ESTHER 7:2–8

On the second day, the king again asked Esther at the wine feast, "What is your wish, Queen Esther? It shall be granted you. And what is your request? Even to half the kingdom, it shall be fulfilled." Queen Esther replied: "If Your Majesty will do me the favor, and if it pleases Your Majesty, let my life be granted me as my wish, and my people as my request. For we have been sold, my people and I, to be destroyed, massacred, and exterminated. Had we only been sold as bondmen and bondwomen, I would have kept silent; for the adversary is not worthy of the king's trouble."

Thereupon King Ahasuerus demanded of Queen Esther. "Who is he and where is he who dared to do this?" "The adversary and enemy," replied Esther, "is this evil Haman!" And Haman cringed in terror before the king and the queen. The king, in his fury, left the wine feast for the palace garden, while Haman remained to plead with Queen Esther for his life; for he saw that the king had resolved to destroy him. When the king returned from the palace garden to the banquet room, Haman was lying prostrate on the couch on which Esther reclined. "Does he mean," cried the king, "to ravish the queen in my own palace?"

COMMENTARY

Esther makes us confront what we think when we think about the nature of biblical heroes. Do we prefer them to be entirely virtuous? Or do we feel more inspired by an ordinary human mixture of qualities that these heroes, wrestling and suffering, take in hand in service to a desired goal? When they achieve the goal, they do so by striving against their own lesser qualities.

Clearly the Bible prefers the second way. Of its heroes and heroines, none is without flaw. Think of preening Joseph, duplicitous Jacob, lascivious David, irascible Moses; cruel Sarah, manipulative Rebekah, thieving Rachel—all of those who grow despite, or dragging, their flaws toward greatness.

Esther is of their company. She makes no protest against the lulling, dulling attentions she receives as she prepares to become winner of the harem beauty contest (for months, rubbed with lotions, soaked in perfumes). She may, in short, have in her at the beginning a good deal of empty-headed narcissist, of silly girl who thinks of nothing but her skin. Yet once chosen queen, she is able, at risk of death, to throw her whole being into combat against the forces of evil. She resembles some of our contemporaries, so disquieting to preconceptions of what thinking, valorous women ought to look like: the ones who insist on dyeing, teasing, and spray-fixing their hair, who wear sexy clothes, stiletto heels, grow inch-long fingernails lacquered red; and just when they've convinced you they haven't a bean worth saving in their brains, send themselves through law school, medical school, Ph.D. programs, and come out fighting for righteous causes, still wearing three-inch heels.

I have never met a woman who liked the Megillah of Esther. Too many aspects of the story make us squirm.

First, what to do with Vashti? She seems a heroine of defiance, but the text doesn't recognize her. It's the genius of the midrashic rabbis that adds the essential note missing from Vashti's part of the story. When the King sent for her to appear before his carousing guests, says a midrash in *Pirke de Rabbi Eliezer,* she was to come naked.

Every Purim I have to check the text to remind myself that this searing detail is not in the Bible story. But the midrashic version, once imagined, will not go away. It has seized the text, and made itself a legitimate part of it.

The rabbis did not say that Vashti was a hero, but they heightened our sense of what was at stake for her. She was not arrogant and willful, she was self-respecting and full of courage. She upholds the sacredness of human, therefore divine, aspect in a court so debauched that any woman who enters will certainly be dehumanized.

Into this milieu Mordecai thrusts his niece, Esther. Mordecai doesn't yet have the excuse that the Jews are threatened. Haman has still not spoken. But just in case the time comes. And when it does, Esther turns herself into a great and heroic strategist—albeit of the bedroom.

With uneasiness we see that the text praises Esther but is silent on Vashti, and silent on the part Mordecai plays when he volunteers Esther for the King's harem.

Esther is a Purim-shpiel, a play, and all of our Purim celebrations are playful. Yet beneath the surface of the story are underlying layers of story to which we also respond. The thrusting of Esther into whoredom by her uncle can't be entirely dismissed as cartoon, considering the history of women in the world. And the threat of annihilation of the Jews is too present in our history, recent and ancient, for us to regard the Megillah as entirely playful.

Then there is the killing orgy at the end.

The great massacre of Haman's family and the Shushan populace (all of whom are anti-Semites) is folk hyperbole, a release of frustration and wish fulfillment at Jewish powerlessness. But the Purim massacre of Palestinian worshipers at a mosque in Hebron some years ago by a literalist of *Megillat Ester* conflates reality and dream, folklore and fact, harmless wish-fulfilling fantasy and hideous deed. Yet even before we ever heard of that massacre, we felt in the story of Esther a built-in unease, an instability, as the reader, or hearer, registers these undercurrents.

When Vashti's incredibly risky refusal of the King makes way for Esther's obsequiousness, we understand that Vashti is haughty in the service of self-respect and the dignity of personhood, made in God's image; Esther is self-sacrificing in the most self-demeaning way in the service of the Jewish people.

Megillat Ester chooses Esther's way over Vashti's, but surely we'd like to acknowledge the importance of both.

In my own midrashic continuation of the story, "After Esther," I try to.

After Esther

Haman and his sons are dead, hurrah! The Jews are under the protection of King Ahasuerus, who encouraged them to punish the anti-Semites of Shushan. Now people respect the Jews because of their surprising blows. And all this is the work of beautiful and clever Esther, whom the King desired—thank God!—and made his wife!

Now Esther, who saved the Jewish people from annihilation, is left to live out her life with King Ahasuerus. For a while the afterglow of glory gave a lovely light, but then it faded. Esther's husband raised up the Jews, but he's the same Ahasuerus, devoted to drunken revelries, and a sloppy drunk himself much of the time. Whenever Esther sleeps she dreams escape dreams.

One night the inevitable happens. Ahasuerus throws a lavish, wine-soaked saturnalia for powerful neighboring potentates. Some rule kingdoms wealthier than his. Some boast more renowned magicians. Some brag of the extraordinary beauty of their women. In that category, King Ahasuerus feels no disadvantage. His queen, he says, can be compared to the finest woman on earth.

"Prove it," yell the swaying, sousing, lolling, vomiting potentates.

At that moment, Esther is dreaming one of her escape dreams. It is set in another time and land whose language is incomprehensible to her, as if she's being prepared for other lives.

This other Esther steps onto a brilliantly lit stage, wearing red spike heels and a white bathing suit with a no-string bra and a G-string bikini bottom.

"What's holding things up?" leers a man with a tape measure.

This Esther tells him to watch where he lays his tape.

He yells out the numbers: "38-22-38! She's a perfect contender!" He gives her a friendly nudge on the thigh and asks for her hobby.

This Esther says she has no hobby.

"Sing with a guitar, dance on your toes, strum a little on a harp?" She could sing 'Mary Had a Little Lamb,' for God's sake, couldn't she?

Esther has never tried. She is usually quiet, by herself, an orphan, she explains. The reason she entered a beauty contest was to be of help to her people.

"That's the ticket! You tell 'em! They love to hear that stuff!"

He's right. There isn't a dry eye in the house when Esther is crowned. The tapeman himself sets the crown on her head. As his hands come down he brushes them against her, top and bottom. Then he's on to the runner-up. Esther sees her fight to keep her smile as he rummages among the trophies on a table with one hand and rummages behind the runner-up's back with the other.

This Esther removes her shoe and, with her heel, spikes

his hand to the table. "I thought of a hobby," she says. "Tabletop ornaments."

By the time Esther wakes from the dream the King sends six eunuchs to tell Esther to anoint and perfume herself for three days and then appear before the visiting potentates—naked! The eunuchs laugh: "Esther's royal share/now laid bare!"

Esther fasts and prays and scours her clever brain for a plan, a strategy. She runs to the window to look into the courtyard, hoping Mordecai will be there, but he's gone. He moved with his wife and children to the suburbs now that the anti-Semites are letting in the Jews.

Toward dawn of the first night she falls asleep and dreams again. Isn't this strange, she thinks in the dream. Here I am a queen and have everything, why am I weeping?

In fact this dream is the strangest of all. She sees a crowd of people celebrating, dressed in costumes to resemble herself, Vashti, and Mordecai. From this throng of Esthers and Vashtis and Mordecais emerge three people who really are Esther and Vashti and Mordecai, and they begin to speak.

Vashti wears a shift on which is printed *Jews for Vashti*. She says, "There is a Vashti faction, you know. They regard me as the heroine of the story, not you."

"I always thought you were brave," answers Esther.

"I deliberately usurped myself. When I refused to submit to the King I made room for you to be chosen," says Vashti.

"The Kingdom was filled with beautiful virgins!" Esther says. "How did it happen that the King chose me?"

"Indeed, the Persians scorn Jewish women. Beauty spoiled by suffering, they say. I was the one who accustomed the King to such beauty. In Esther he recognized Vashti and looked for me in your arms!"

"Then you, Vashti—are you . . .?"

"Let it be enough to say that I created the taste in Ahasuerus for the sad-eyed look of suffering Jewish beauty. He couldn't get enough of it, as good as bound feet to a Mandarin."

"But poor Vashti, you were banished!"

"I was the spy who did not come in from the cold."

"And poor Esther has come in from the cold, but to the heat of Hell."

"When they rubbed your body with oils and perfumes for a year you were content! Rubbed, massaged, perfumed, painted with colors, to win the King's notice. Ah, life in the seraglio! Lying on cushions, feeding on sweets. Soft airs, warm vapors, lulling songs, sleep, dreams. Admit it—you were delighted with those comforts and attentions!"

"The mind is meant to rot there!" Esther weeps. "In the night, terror and disgust. Submitting to the wine-soaked flesh of my husband. Sinking into nothingness, a kind of madness! Then Mordecai came to me. 'Don't think, Esther, because you're a queen, that you can escape the common fate,' he said. From that moment my brain burned in its shell. Like a general I maneuvered the two men! Lulled Haman, positioned Ahasuerus, then planted poison seeds of fear in Haman until he threw himself on my mercy while the king read in Haman's outstretched limbs not fear but lust! Action was my freedom! I never foresaw prison."

Then Mordecai, wearing the sackcloth and ashes of permanent mourning, joins in.

"Stop! It's indecent for you both to mourn your own tiny fate. If it's clearly for the good of the people, can't a Jewish girl be sacrificed without such hullabaloo? Didn't Abraham agree to sacrifice Isaac? The boy lay there, trussed, until an angel freed him. My girl wiggled free of her bonds and saved the Jewish people! Should I be blamed for that? These quibbles eat away at heroism. And then the bloodbath at the end. Yes, I'll call it by its true name. Massacre. The Jews, unarmed, were to have been slaughtered. Once armed, they did the slaughtering. Does that surprise anyone? I get bags of hate mail, imagine, over such a story! For once, Jews come out winners, and nobody can stand it."

A note flies in attached to a brick, just missing Mordecai's head. He picks it up, and reads.

"Another humanitarian who threatens to kill me because I condone killing!" He shouts, "It offends you? Believe me, it doesn't offend me. Were you upset by the Nazi hangings at Nuremberg? Not me! I regretted every one who took his own life—Hitler, Goebbels, Goering—cheating the hangman. Mussolini upside down by the feet in the public square—that was a moment!

" 'But Haman's sons,' people say, 'how does it look? Couldn't they be spared?' In that case, I say, Get them to hand over *The Protocols of the Elders of Zion!* Their pamphlets on how Jews run the media and control banking, their Ku Klux Klan hoods, their swastika armbands, their true-eyewitness accounts of the murder of children whose blood is baked in the matzoh, their cache of arms and crosses for burning, their Wannsee agreement, their final solution—all of it! Then I'll think it over."

Dream-Esther astonishes the Esther who is dreaming by what she now cries out: "Storytellers say it never happened, that I never had sex with the King. That God in His mercy intervened, caused the necessary organ to wither at the moment of penetration, or so pickled it in brine that with it at one end, and the King's pickled brain at the other, they failed between them to capture the place of entry. Night after night. Forever, they say. Some people want to believe that. But if they thought about it, they would realize the truth. How much can we call on God to do in one miracle? And if great, widespread tragedy is averted, isn't it too petty, too ungrateful, to ask, "And now what about my personal happiness?" That's how it is with us. We move from cataclysm to cataclysm. History rewards us with tableaux. Haman is forever plotting, Mordecai and Esther are forever racking their brains for a way out, the Jews are forever oppressed, then they are triumphant. I stand forever looking out of the palace window with longing in my heart."

As soon as she wakes on the second day, Esther knows what to do. She sends a swift message to the Jews of Shushan, who are now prosperous and safe because of her.

"Ransom me," her note says. "Offer any sum to the King for my release. He'll be glad to be rid of me—there's a limit to how much suffering Jewish beauty he can take. Let me live in quiet peace among my people. Remember that my silence and submission have been for your sake."

But the elders of the community, who now feel extremely safe, say, "How women love to catastrophize! She's the queen. Let her make use of her own wealth to ransom herself!"

Among the beggar throngs outside the palace gates are spies and augurs, all of them watchful. News of this new scandal in the making at court soon spreads among the tattered multitude and reaches the ears of Vashti, who survives among them on palace scraps.

As soon as Vashti hears the whispers, she slides into the palace along secret passageways known to her. In rags, her hair a wilderness, with all the signs of decay—scabrous skin and toothless gums—upon her, she makes her way to Esther's chamber. There she finds the queen collapsed in terror, under the contemptuous eyes of the six eunuchs, whose gelded bodies are clothed with rich garments.

"Did you think," Vashti says, "because you were Queen, that you could escape the fate of women? It may even be that you were put here for this purpose—to take your stand against our destroyers!"

"But if I refuse," Esther answers, "I will be destroyed like you!"

The six eunuchs jeer together in their terrible doggerel: "Vashti, Vashti,/balked because she/had pride!/Now Death's at her side!"

And they hold their noses because Vashti's dignity led directly to her poverty and smells bad. The eunuchs throw her out.

"Help me, God," Esther prays. "Free my wits to improvise a plan, or send Mordecai to advise me, or let the King think of the Chronicles again, and for the sake of past favors, rescind his decree against me now."

But not one of these things happens. History, like literature, doesn't like to wade in the same solution twice.

That night the six grinning eunuchs carry out the command of King Ahasuerus to bring Esther forth naked. "Esther, Esther," they maliciously recite, "this'll test 'er!"

Esther removes her rich garments one by one. When she is naked, barefoot, and crownless, she walks silently along the palace corridors flanked by the eunuchs.

As they approach the hall where the king carouses with his guests, she hears rough shouts, bursts of laughter, and now and then the stifled scream of a woman.

But I am Queen! Then Esther thinks of the women in her dream who put on silver paper crowns and called themselves Queen Esther. She looks down at her bare feet and knows her power is spent.

On the hip of a guard hangs a jeweled dagger. Esther snatches it and plunges it into her chest. Soon her own blood clothes her naked body in a royal garment of red, and under this covering the eunuchs carry beautiful Esther into the King's presence.

Some say he was remorseful, shoved his weeping face into an armpit while his huge belly shook with grief; some say enraged—he threw wine goblets and food at the eunuchs; some say delighted to have won his bet and rid himself of his tiresome wife at the same time. He clapped his hands, struggled to his feet and skipped elephantiacally around the room, like the hippo toe-dancing in Disney's *Fantasia*.

When Mordecai heard the news he put on sackcloth and ashes again. He always kept them handy—what a pessimist!

"Oh, Esther," he grieved. "Just a few more years of suffering and you might have become a *tzadeket!* Now that can't happen, and the Jews no longer have a friend at court. Any day the evil decree against us may be revived."

And so it came to pass. Again and again. For Queen Esther was dead. No one had thought it necessary to protect the protectress, or to grant the Jewish woman whom we call Queen her freedom.

Contemporary Women Look at Biblical Women

RUTH AND NAOMI

RUTH 3–19

Elimelech, Naomi's husband, died; and she was left with her two sons. They married Moabite women, one named Orpah and the other Ruth, and they lived there about ten years. Then those two—Mahlon and Chilion—also died; so the woman was left without her two sons and without her husband.

She started out with her daughters-in-law to return from the country of Moab; for in the country of Moab she had heard that the Lord had taken note of His people and given them food. Accompanied by her two daughters-in-law, she left the place where she had been living; and they set out on the road back to Judah.

But Naomi said to her two daughters-in-law, "Turn back, each of you to her mother's house. May the Lord deal kindly with you, as you have dealt with the dead and with me! May the Lord grant that each of you find security in the house of a husband!" And she kissed them farewell. They broke into weeping and said to her, "No, we will return with you to your people."

But Naomi replied, "Turn back, my daughters! Why should you go with me? Have I any more sons in my body who might be husbands for you? Turn back, my daughters, for I am too old to be married. Even if I thought there was hope for me, even if I were married tonight and I also bore sons, should you wait for them to grow up? Should you on their account debar yourselves from marriage? Oh, no, my daughters! My lot is far more bitter than yours, for the hand of the Lord has struck out against me."

They broke into weeping again, and Orpah kissed her mother-in-law farewell. But Ruth clung to her. So she said, "See, your sister-in-law has returned to her people and her gods. Go follow your sister-in-law." But Ruth replied, "Do not urge me to leave you, to turn back and not follow you. For wherever you go, I will go; wherever you lodge, I will lodge; your people shall be my people, and your God my God. Where you die I will die, and there I will be buried. Thus and more may the Lord do to me if anything but death parts me from you." When Naomi saw how determined she was to go with her, she ceased to argue with her; and the two went on until they reached Bethlehem.

COMMENTARY

The story of Ruth and Naomi is beloved around the world—by Christians as well as Jews, by men as well as women. Yet even this story of lives reborn from ruin, of happiness snatched from misery, of human goodness and mercy that bring about human renewal, can, when looked at with an unflinching contemporary eye, show itself vulnerable to gaps, schisms, holes in the fabric of narrative through which our willing suspension of disbelief may seep away. We can turn away from the story indifferently. "Yes, yes," we say, "another tale of a good girl who did as she was told and in the end earned herself a life of security."

There are questions the text forces upon us. In my view, unless we face up to them we cannot open ourselves to the beauty of *The Book of Ruth.* Was Ruth really not very bright, a passively acquiescent girl? Was Naomi loving or manipulative? Was the whole ethos of "acquiring" land and a woman so demeaning as to make any talk of heroism ludicrous? Unless we first work through our skepticism and ironies, we cannot come upon Ruth in a new way, a way that suits us now, with all our contemporary questions.

Only after such "working through"—and the first three sections of my midrash play, "Dialogues on Devotion," are that—can we come closer to admitting how much we lack, in our contemporary lives, the openness to virtue and self-forgetting love that the text enthrones.

In the final section of the dialogues, five contemporary women, having hurled at the text every accusation they can think of, admit their need and their longing to embrace our lost absolutes of goodness, kindness, and unironic virtue.

I place their discussion last because the progression of their dialogues, moving as they do from alienation and adversarial questioning to the need (and the expressed longing) to draw close to some affirmation, summarizes for me the aspect of the contemporary woman's engagement with Bible text I have most wanted to address in this volume: the effort to reenter Jewish texts without sacrifice of contemporary selfhood.

Dialogues on Devotion

SCENE:

Five women, their ages spanning the decades from late twenties to fifties, are meeting in a Manhattan living room of one of their number. It is early evening; they have carried coffee to chairs and sofa. Comfortable with one another, they are members of an ongoing group facetiously acronymed WGTDTB: "Women Gathered to Deplore the Bible." One or two of them secretly wish the initials more innocently connoted "Women Gathered to Discuss the Bible." However, when mailings first went out under the latter rubric, too few responded.

CHARACTERS:

SHARON, the oldest, a psychologist. The meeting is in her apartment. According to their informal custom, the hostess acts as a kind of moderator. The others are BECKY, LAURA, MARION, AND EVELYN, the youngest. Each is a member of a profession—social worker, lawyer, history professor, and doctoral candidate in English literature. All received religious school training in childhood; a few still read Hebrew. All, in adulthood, recognize with pain that their training overlooked the fact that the bias of the Bible was masculine and they were female. The same blankness characterized the way, in secular schools, they were taught great works of English literature: a teaching that never acknowledged that many of the works were anti-Semitic, and that they, the students, were Jews.

In each section there are two speakers in dialogue, the others acting as chorus. The scene should be visualized with speakers sitting in bright reading light, the others in dimmer light, which brightens when they speak.

1. Letting Off Steam: Sharon and Becky

SHARON (*glancing around*): It's a shame we're so few this month, because *The Book of Ruth* is so . . . *(interrupting herself to joke.)* Well, maybe the others didn't come because Ruth's not a book they like to deplore. It's one of the very few where we finally get some good lines! And they really are good lines, aren't they? *(Declaims)* "Wherever you go I will go!"

CHORUS (*voices tinged with satire, speaking one at a time*):

—"Your people will be my people!"

—"Your God will be my God!"

—"Where you die I will die!"

—Yes, indeed!

BECKY: Of course we know there isn't a single man portrayed in the Bible without a blemish, not even Moses. Unfortunately, when it comes to Ruth, she has to be dehumanized into someone who's always unselfish, loyal, and in perfect control of herself.

SHARON: I'm surprised to hear you say that, Becky. I always felt you were someone who believed that people were basically good. Isn't that why you became a social worker, after all?

BECKY: I think people would be good if circumstances allowed them to be—don't you?

SHARON: Maybe. In any case, it takes extraordinary people to be good when circumstances aren't especially conducive. For the sake of fairness to the story, we have to say that *everyone* here is virtuous, especially Boaz! And I admit I love the virtue of Boaz, though I find Ruth's tiresome. I suppose I could try to analyze why that's so, but I think I'll just ease into this slowly, tonight.

BECKY: Anyway, for once it's women who make the story move, yet they still need men to redeem the property, to redeem them. Boaz even says (*she consults one of the books open on a small table beside her chair*) yes—here it is: He will "buy" Ruth along with the property! This other translation doesn't use the word buy. It says "acquire." That's splitting hairs.

SHARON: If you're looking for faults, Ruth has them, though the Bible doesn't count them as faults. You could just as easily describe Ruth as passive, subservient, waiting to be reclaimed—bought—however you translate! I still want to be fair, though. In those days progeny and family affiliation really *were* the most important things in life.

CHORUS: —Speaking of important things—I can't stay late! I have a law brief to write!

—I have my students' papers to read!

—I have my orals to prepare for!

SHARON: We'll just have to speed things up, that's all—but it's a complex story! We already have two conflicting sets of defining qualities for Ruth. Is she a symbol of passive, unquestioning virtue or a brave partner in adventure? A third pattern suggests itself, variant of a folk tale. Mother and daughter-in-law set out into the world to seek their fortune, defenseless, like Hansel and Gretel. Will they meet a witch who wants to eat them? No, they meet a dear, grandfatherly man who feeds them.

BECKY: Not exactly out into the world, though. Back to Naomi's home, though she's been away long enough to feel a stranger. Her husband, an important man, dragged her and the kids out to Moab when there was famine in their own land. How will the folks at home feel about her coming back now that things have improved in Judah? Oddly enough, the folks at home don't seem to resent it at all. They don't say sarcastically, "Well, Naomi, so you've decided to come back to us now that there's food on the table!" They say, "Is this Naomi?" Everyone's incredibly forbearing. Where do you find people like that? In the Bible, I suppose. But don't we need to make some connection to ourselves here? Right away, Naomi tells them *her* troubles. Never mind how many of their children died in the famine! The text leaves that out. In fact, the text leaves too much out. I can't connect with this story unless we put a few things back.

SHARON: Shouldn't we try to follow the chronology of this so-called simple tale?

BECKY: All right, but first I want to say it's a story I do not trust.

SHARON: Don't *trust* it? Why?

BECKY: The whole world takes this story to its heart. But only because it leaves out reality principles. Like nastiness, I'm sorry to say. And ulterior motives. Spend a day with any of the families in my caseload!

CHORUS: —Spend a day with me in any courtroom!

—Spend a day in the History Department of my university.

—Or the English Department of mine!

SHARON: Spend a day in my therapy office! But you haven't stopped believing that virtue is also part of reality, have you?

BECKY: No, of course not. But Ruth makes me aware of the devil lurking behind the lines. Naomi says, "Go, my daughter, to the gleaning in the fields." Later we get a good idea of what the dangers are, when Boaz tells his workers not to harm Ruth, the unprotected female. So in what spirit does Naomi send Ruth out on these errands?

SHARON: Now you make it sound as if Naomi is sending Ruth to destruction, deceiving Ruth the way Abraham deceived Isaac. Do you really think that the minute you get a parent-child story, somewhere there's a sacrifice? Another *Akedah?* I can't believe the goodness of the story doesn't move you!

BECKY: Of course it moves me—that's why I don't trust it! It's trying to put me to sleep, like all stories about virtuous women! I'm not speaking as a social worker, I'm speaking as myself. I can't afford it. Part of me would love to go into that world and close the door! Such a lovely world, where people behave like ideal beings. But maybe that's going too far, calling them ideal beings, when all that's on their mind is procreation and property!

SHARON: What about Ruth's loyalty to Naomi? What about Naomi's concern for Ruth? What about Boaz's respect for Ruth's goodness toward her mother-in-law? That's not just procreation and property!

BECKY: A young woman gives herself to an old man in exchange for food. That teaches us something about female survival. On the other hand, more than anything, it's a story of redemption! Of the property of a widowed woman, and of life, through acts of unselfishness and virtue. I know I keep going around and around myself here. But I don't think it's entirely my fault. There's great beauty and virtue in the story, and there's great ugliness and shame.

SHARON: Yes, I agree we can't get away from the double reading. There's the positive one, but what we also get is female subjugation and humiliation. Boaz's warning to his men in the fields only points up the terrors that must have been the usual thing. In that world women had to be pragmatists. Naomi's husband and sons have died—ah! we're finally coming to chronology—so she calls herself empty, meaning her womb. She's too old to bear again. Her daughters-in-law can still bear sons, and she tells them, "Go back to your families, hurry up and get fixed up with new husbands, don't hang around with me, I'm finished!" Well, where *could* a woman go in those biblical days, what could she have, without the protection of a man? Nowhere. Nada. The daughters-in-law have to find new husbands and have sons.

That's their function, their whole value in that society. Why should that make us feel bitter? Things have changed!

BECKY: *The Book of Ruth* talks about taking possession of women and of property. If Ruth weren't a widow, her virginity would be very much to the point. As it is, her virtue is attested to, if I remember, by her having stuck close to Naomi. In fact, Boaz comments that Ruth has not been fooling around with the young men in the field. Nobody gives sexual purity credentials to the other possible redeemer or to Boaz, either. Is *Boaz* a widower? Does *he* have children? Does *he* fool around with gleaners in the fields? The text doesn't bother to record any of that. And we tell ourselves how much things have changed!

CHORUS: —How can we speak of change?

—Nothing has really changed!

—And the text doesn't even bother to tell . . .

—Oh, those texts, they're hopelessly fragmented, garbled . . .

—And framed to keep women in line . . .

—Or worse, not in line at all. *Out* of line, pariahs, actually warned against!

—Why do we bother, what is the point?

SHARON (*standing*): I hope we'll find one, after we take a break to get more coffee or tea. There are themes we haven't touched yet!

2. Seeing the Loss: Sharon and Laura

LAURA: Sharon, you'd like us to be chronological, so let's go back to leaving Moab. But I think we should be very strict with the text. It wouldn't hurt to read the fine print. Ruth says her piece, "Where you go, I go," and all that. Then she adds something very strange. She says: "Your God will be my God." Now, Naomi has just judged God very harshly. She says *(checks her book)*, "My lot is far more bitter than yours, for the hand of the Lord has struck out against me." So why, at this moment, should Ruth proclaim allegiance to a God that even Naomi seems to be withdrawing from? Even more important, why, at this moment, is she so *tactless* as to mention God at all, when she knows what a painful point it is for Naomi? Why should Ruth in effect be saying, "Now that I see how cruelly your God has treated you, I will follow your God"?

SHARON: But sense or no sense, when Ruth does say that, it's a stunning moment. Naomi, follower of God, has just all but denounced God, and look!—a young woman with choices chooses Naomi's God!

LAURA: I don't think she does choose Naomi's God—not yet. The way I read Ruth's statement is like this: "You and I," she is saying to Naomi, "have loved the same people for so many years, and then suffered their loss together. My emotional life is bound up with yours. I can't *see* any other life for myself than with you, and that includes, for better or worse, even staying with the God I now hear you denounce. Your God will be my God, and if we must denounce God, we will do it together." Ruth then adds,

"Where you die, I will die, and there I will be buried." She may actually expect, as the remnant of this ill-fated family, that she and Naomi will both be struck dead next! Though Ruth's bravery at that moment is extraordinary, I see her embracing "Naomi's God" not out of love of God at all—how could she?—rather with a kind of existential stoicism. And it is this stoical going on, this determination to bestow human kindness in a world blasted by God, that gives Ruth greatness.

SHARON: So Ruth and Naomi go back in resignation, possibly expecting more terror from this punishing God, you think? Naomi then figures something out to get them food, the way Elimelech had figured something out before, when there was famine and he took his family to Moab. People act, and no one knows ahead of time whether God will smile on those actions or not. In Naomi's case, God does smile, after a while. As God smiled on Abraham and Joseph and Jacob, who also left the land when there was famine. Poor Elimelech doesn't get smiled on, he dies.

LAURA: The commentators love to do what I call their backstitching must-have-beens. They slip in that Elimelech *must have been* a stingy man who didn't want to share his wealth in hard times, so he went to Moab, and God zapped him and his sons. This is the sort of commentary that makes me want to sue for libel! Ishmael *must have been* shooting arrows into people, that's why Sarah wanted him out of the house; Cain's sacrifice to God *must have been* done in the wrong spirit, that's why God rejected it, and on and on—apologetics for God. Better to have commentaries that tell the truth. Job's truth and Naomi's truth. Elimelech tried his best and died. Cain's sacrifice was as good as Abel's, Ishmael was a boy like Isaac or any other boy, Elimelech did what Abraham, Joseph, and Jacob all did—went to another land when there was famine. "I will be gracious to whom I will be gracious to," God said to Moses. Weren't the commentators listening? With their pietistic interpretations, their zeal to teach a moral order, they brought themselves to the absurdity of saying that everything bad that happened was punishment for sin. And where is existential chanciness then? As post-Holocaust Jews, we haven't the right to say Naomi's plans are rewarded because they are *better* plans than Elimelech's. We should symbolically empty ten drops of wine from our glass of joy at Naomi's triumph, and remember what befell people of virtue and ingenuity who by prayer or plan struggled to save themselves and their little ones, but earned no protection from God.

SHARON: But for now, for Naomi and Ruth, can't we agree, at least, that things worked out? It's a story of Jewish rebirth after terrible suffering. Symbolized, as in Job, with a new family. God gives no answer to the question of why such suffering happened. Just—start again. Nature's answer and God's answer turn out to be exactly the same. Start again with fresh-planted seed. That's why I think we should address the two characters in the story who "defect," so to say. The other daughter-in-law, Orpah, who doesn't come with Naomi, and later the other male relative who won't redeem. The defecting male relative creates a certain narrative suspense: *Will Boaz get his turn to redeem?* But Orpah does nothing for the narrative line, except, of course, to lighten it. One daughter-in-law less to schlep back to the land of Judah.

LAURA: What if Orpah *had* also gone back with Naomi? Then we might have had a Leah and Rachel situation between sisters-in-law or sisters, whichever they were. At the end, people say to Boaz, "May the Lord make the woman who is coming into your house"—meaning Ruth—"like Rachel and Leah." That almost looks as if the two, Orpah and Ruth, were meant to come back. Boaz, old as he is, would take both widows as wives. Ruth produces the line that leads to King David, and Orpah to—let's see . . . I know there's a legend that Goliath was a descendant of Orpah and her new Moabite husband. Doesn't that sound like what might have happened if she'd married Boaz, carrying out the traditional pairing of enemies issuing from the same father, like Isaac and Ishmael, or Jacob and Esau, or Joseph and his brothers? Or, wait—why couldn't Orpah have borne a *daughter* to Boaz? From her descends Queen X! She, too, turns out to be a wonderful psalmist. It's those Moabite genes! After David seduces Uriah's wife, Nathan the prophet ought to tell David that God is deposing him from kingship the way God deposed Saul when he displeased God. Queen X is anointed in David's place, ruling more justly than David. She doesn't seduce anyone's wife!

SHARON: Instead of that, Orpah and the defecting redeemer lose their places in the story. The man who won't redeem is never named at all, and Orpah is merely not-Ruth. I can just hear Orpah complaining to her therapist. "Why is it other people know when to say yes or no and I never do? I'm always on the wrong foot! Why couldn't *I* have gone with Naomi instead of Ruth? You know why? Because I always felt Naomi favored *Ruth's* husband, not mine, but I should have gone anyway! Why am I always putting myself down? Why do I let other people write the script for me?"

LAURA: Those two defectors sound like people I know, myself. Maybe I'm even one of them. I pride myself on being able to think through the logic of a situation and not let emotion carry me away. I want to behave decently, but not be a self-sacrificer. In short, not my mother. All of a sudden, I think the story is saying that logic and practicality aren't enough. You need something closer to passionate generosity, to more-than-enough, to reasons of the heart, not the head.

SHARON: Is this the legal mind of Laura speaking? Anyway, I gather neither of us would have wanted to be Orpah. How about Ruth? Speaking for myself, I'd like to have her serenity, her sense of doing her best for what she chose.

LAURA: Back to your mother and father or stick to your mother-in-law, and no such thing as going it alone? You call those choices?

SHARON: But look what these women can do with their nonchoices! At the end, people say to Boaz, "May your house be like the house of Perez whom Tamar bore to Judah." So the text invites us to pair Ruth and Tamar, two women who dove into the adventure of their own stories and made themselves part of history.

LAURA: It's true that both Tamar and Ruth lure older men into impregnating them. But unlike Tamar's father-in-law Judah, Naomi can't impregnate her daughter-in-law.

Maybe we ought to say that Boaz is Naomi's chosen surrogate!

SHARON: Now you want us to think of Naomi as Judah in drag?

LAURA: Look at it this way—Tamar is both the inventor of her own story and its passionate actor. In *Ruth,* inventor and actor are divided between two women. Naomi is the brilliant strategist—what a trial lawyer she would have made! Ruth acts. Tamar was obsessed with having progeny, if necessary even with her father-in-law. Ruth is obsessed with being with her mother-in-law, who is obsessed by her grief at being "empty." Naomi finds a way to fulfill covenant with a "covenanted" relative, someone in the circle of family redeemers. She can fill up her own emptiness through Ruth's child and find safety for Ruth in Boaz's house. It's a dramatic summing-up!

SHARON: One thing I keep coming back to—in biblical life, it's progeny and inheritance that count. Family clusters are only beads on the covenantal string. From this Jewish string of beads God chooses, here and there, a Moses, an Abraham, a Sarah, a Rebekah, a Tamar, a Naomi, a who knows what next? At least the sense of stretching futureward is a change from Eastern thought, where the tragic wheel of life rolls its cycles over each generation till it, too, is broken.

LAURA: Broken strings of beads are no less terrible than wheels! Creatures capable of comprehending their own tragedy deserve better. On the other hand, if we hadn't been given tragedy for our lot—if we had, say, eternal lives or eternally bland ones—we wouldn't have *The Book of Ruth,* would we? No death, no poetry. No legal system, either.

SHARON: I'm not as stoical as you, Laura. I find it interesting—comforting, I suppose I really mean—to think of the Kabbalist view here and set it beside the view of a deity in full charge of things. Creation is broken. God is shattered into the ten *sephirot*—attributes. God takes up residence in one, then another, then another. Like the old Jewish joke-curse, do you know it? May you be a millionaire and own beautiful mansions?

LAURA: How it that a curse?

SHARON: Ah-ha, wait! And in each mansion, may there be spacious rooms, gorgeously furnished, with luxurious beds.

LAURA: What's bad about that? Who wouldn't take it? Come on, drop the shoe!

SHARON: And may you go from mansion to mansion, from luxurious bed to bed, turning and tossing, unable to sleep!

LAURA: Thank you! Wait a minute, you think that's what God is doing?

SHARON: I exaggerate. But the Kabbalist idea does divide God into personae—wisdom, mercy, justice, judgment, pity, and all the rest, some of them male and some female. It's up to human beings to bring those attributes into a single focus, like some giant stereoptican. By virtue, by goodness, by fulfilling the law. And that ties in with why it's important for the characters in *Ruth* to choose the right way. Those who act out a vigorous virtue can alter the world. Besides, the Kabbalist idea is sexy, too. God in the male mode has intercourse with the female element, the *Shechina,* to achieve Oneness. Look how important the female is! And that, in a way, is what Ruth is about, too. *Imitatio Dei* on the humblest, threshing-floor level.

LAURA: Is this what you mean by a *hopeful* idea? Thinking of God in pieces? I have to tell you that I find that really depressing! Not to mention pagan!

CHORUS: —Most views of God are depressing.

—And avoiding the pagan is as skittery as balancing on a skateboard!

—Either God is responsible for evil . . .

—Which is depressing . . .

—Or some other force, like the Devil, is responsible for evil . . .

—Which is probably pagan . . .

—It's certainly not a monotheistic idea . . .

—And it's still depressing!

SHARON (*standing*): Maybe it's time to take another tiny little break? Stretch, move around the room? A little liqueur? It's a harvest festival, after all. Have some fruit! *(She takes up a platter and moves about the circle.)*

3. Mother-Daughter: Sharon and Marion

MARION: Sharon, for all your efforts, you deserve a little more chronology! I am also going back to the beginning to ask two questions. The first is, What would we say if Naomi weren't a mother-in-law but a mother?

SHARON (*laughing*): We'd say, "Doesn't Ruth know about the importance of separating from the mother, of developing an autonomous life?" We'd quote Margaret Mahler! We'd say, "Ruth was led by the nose! When does she develop a will and purpose of her own, instead of going wherever her mother goes!"

MARION: Here's the second question, and it goes back even farther. Had the daughters-in-law gone on worshipping their own gods all the time they were married to Naomi's sons? Laura's commentary backstitchers probably say somewhere that a virtuous woman like Ruth *must have been* converted to God already. But Naomi tells Ruth, "Your sister-in-law has returned to her gods. Go follow your sister-in-law." Why would one daughter-in-law convert and not the other? That's unlikely. And if Ruth *had* converted, would Naomi be so wicked as to urge her back to pagan gods in Moab? No—Ruth has either gone on worshipping her pagan gods all during her marriage, or she's been indifferent to religion altogether—recognizable to some of us! Ruth shows tact by not saying to Naomi, "Your God has given us no protection, why don't we try the ones they've got back in Moab?"

SHARON: Personally, I worry a bit about Ruth's family. Won't her own mother be hurt when she hears? This is a problem for Becky's family caseworker all over again! How old is Ruth, anyway? Childbearing age, that's all we know. Maybe a teenager? The culture was different, but some things may not have changed. We know the pull of other people's mothers, more attractive than our own. Relations with ours are too complicated. Come to think of it, I don't believe there's a single scene of mother-daughter relationship in the entire Bible!

MARION: This one wouldn't be there either, probably, if they weren't trying to say something about tolerance for conversion. Ruth's a Moabite. Historically we should place this just after the Babylonian exile. Some wanted Jewish men to abandon their non-Jewish wives before coming back to Jerusalem. This is a counterbalancing voice. I suppose that says it all, doesn't it! The politics of the day called for a message to go easy on converts. But about helping women like Naomi control their own property, about that the text had nothing to say! As well as anything else to do with furthering the autonomy of women! To think how women have begged for favors, tiny changes in the liturgy that will let them feel a little bit like a covenanted Jew, too—"Oh, please, don't always translate *b'nai Yisrael* as "sons of Israel," please say sons and daughters sometimes, or at least children, oh, please?" It makes me feel sick!

SHARON: Let's not dwell on it, then. Tell me if you agree with a notion I have that Ruth's attraction to a Jewish husband and to somebody else's mother seem to share a certain tendency. It's going toward the genetic outsider, the "Other," as we say. Ruth, the Moabite, seems always attracted outside the immediate "family." That tells me something about her character from the beginning. As a teenager, I myself adored my friends' mothers! Food, sleepovers, shopping trips, all without having to fear or resent too much or too little protectiveness. Friendly detachment—perfect! Naomi reminds me of the mother of the French writer, Colette, who was unable to visit when Colette was ill—she had to watch a rare cactus bloom! Of course, Naomi's distractions are the sorrows of two dead sons, a dead husband. "I left full, I return empty." Since she can't dismiss Ruth, she accepts her coming along, rather listlessly, it seems.

MARION: And that's what's fascinating! Naomi feels almost dead herself. What wakens her to new life? It's not because Ruth loves her! She's far too unsentimental and life-toughened for that. It's because Ruth's presence stirs Naomi to responsibility. "I must find rest for you, my daughter." She thought she could never be a mother again, and then she finds herself taking on a mother's concerns toward needy Ruth! So the text tells us that what keeps people alive is not passively waiting to be loved, but having tasks to perform that require your own love.

SHARON: I see I ought to get my abused women's groups to read Ruth!

MARION: But there's also a dark note here for me. When Naomi does come to life, I find her, frankly, anything but noble. More like controlling and manipulative. Why does she reveal only tiny bits of her plan at a time? Does that show respect for Ruth? Naomi treats Ruth like a dimwit!

SHARON: Couldn't that be because Naomi hasn't herself figured out the whole plan in advance?

MARION: But Naomi *could* have known everything from the start. I have this property, she might have said to herself. I am in deep grief but not destitute. If I can't get a kinsman of my dead husband to redeem my land and my life, I've got this nubile girl to offer. I don't think she's Laura's trial lawyer. She's Robespierre!

SHARON (*laughing*): Madame Defarge and Lady Macbeth come next! But I don't see any of that at all. To me, she really seems without hope and without plan at the beginning. She heads toward home with Ruth, despairing and grief-stricken, she feels it's all hopeless, life has shut down. Gradually on this journey, her despair-frozen brain thaws out. Maybe she's not a brilliant strategist at all, maybe she never reveals everything to Ruth because she herself doesn't know the whole plan in advance! She's trying one piece at a time. Only after Ruth returns successful from each task does Naomi intuit the next. Ruth by chance—by chance? Well, if we can say anything in the Bible is by chance—Ruth gleans in Boaz's field. Then Naomi works out a use for the kinship connection. She tells Ruth to lie on the threshing floor at Boaz's feet and uncover them . . .

CHORUS: —Oh, I remember those feet, those feet!

—We know about patriarchal oaths. Put your hand under my thigh turns out to mean swear on my testicles.

—It shouldn't be too hard to figure out those feet! Feet, knees, thighs, and upward?

MARION: As far as I'm concerned, it's a bold enough act even if they are feet. She gets into Boaz's bed, uncovers a part of him so he'll get cold, wake up, and find her there, where she can declare her kinship and his responsibility. Cover and protect me, she is saying, as your covering warms and protects you. I believe that some Arabs still keep that wedding gesture, the man placing a corner of his cloak over the woman. Notice, though, that Ruth says this to him in his bed at night, not in the field during the day!

SHARON: She's shy. She's modest. Maybe. She also understands perfectly well that Naomi's suggestion is so daring and dangerous that it's not even to be spelled out at this point. As if Naomi is saying, like Macbeth, not Lady Macbeth, "Be ignorant of the deed, dearest chuck!" I think it's generous, not manipulative, of Naomi. If her plan fails, Ruth can save face by saying, "I had no idea what was supposed to happen." Of course there is an incredible intuitive resonance between the two women. Ruth never puts a foot—speaking of feet!—wrong.

MARION: Fine, we disagree. I still say Naomi is orchestrating this, using the only power available to her. When men bully women, women bully their daughters or daughters-in-law. Nowadays, Naomi would write one of those *Cosmopolitan* magazine articles: "Getting your Man to Propose." She thinks daylight doesn't do it. How right she is! It's the *legalities* of the marriage agreement—the levirate marriage, if that's really what it is—that get spelled out in a public way, at the village gate in daylight with witnesses.

SHARON: Yet, that little whispered, nighttime encounter between Boaz and Ruth in bed on the threshing floor is so unbelievably real, it might have happened one minute ago!

MARION: The question is, did they or didn't they have sex? Naomi sent this poor child out with instructions: Go as far as you have to, Ruth, to get what I, Naomi, want!

SHARON: I think that once Boaz remembers there's a nearer redeemer, he gallantly puts his feet, so to say, back in his pocket. So even if no intercourse took place—and there's plenty of ambiguity—the scene already shares the intimacy of marriage, the human one-to-one.

MARION: I'm glad to hear your upbeat view of marriage, Sharon! But we know there's treachery in gleaning fields and threshing floors. Boaz has to warn his male workers not to—wait—*(she opens her book)* yes, this says "molest." "I have ordered the men not to molest you." That's how we know she would have been fair game, an unspoken-for female! How far would they go? Rape? No mother should send a daughter into such danger!

SHARON: But sending Ruth also tells us about alternative dangers. If Ruth *doesn't* go, what would those two women be? Truly empty! Still—you may be right, maybe Naomi is a little detached, maybe more than a little.

MARION: "This may work," thinks Naomi, "or it may not, let's see how far we get." She places Ruth here or there, then moves her somewhere else. Ruth's a chess piece Naomi uses while she plays out her game against Boaz and the other male kinsman, who are such lovely legal redeemers, they'd probably just swallow up Naomi's property if no one was looking.

SHARON: You're saying Ruth's a pawn? For what? No, I really think we're missing . . . look, when Ruth returns from her night on the threshing floor with Boaz, Naomi asks a question. Translations differ. Because the Hebrew is ambiguous, no one can be sure. Some say Naomi asks, "How is it with you, my daughter?" and some say, "Who are you, my daughter?" And both questions are wonderful! Oh, I agree with you a little bit—when Naomi sends Ruth out to Boaz and says, "He will tell you what to do," you might hear an ominous overtone in those words, a combination of the menacing, "*You'll* find out!" and the contemptuous, "Don't ask questions or even think. Be will-less and ignorant, let yourself be abused, if that's what's needed." When Ruth returns, Naomi's question surely means, "How did things go with Boaz?" but she is also asking Ruth a great many other things. It's as if the strong, decisive Naomi is suddenly afraid, and is asking Ruth, "How has all this changed your outer condition? Who are you now? Are you a dishonored woman? A spurned one? Or are you on the way to becoming an honored wife? And how have you changed within yourself? Are you still the open, loving creature you were, or has the experience I made you undergo altered and embittered you forever? Who *are* you now? Still my loving daughter, or my enemy?" What mothers teach, pass on, to their daughters is what daughters come back to confront their mothers with. Naomi's vulnerability to Ruth's answer is as important to me as anything else that happens in the story.

MARION: You make a case for all the meanings of Naomi's question. But the story doesn't stop to unravel them. It hurries on to the near redeemer, to the suspense of whether he will marry Ruth. In the end he doesn't because Ruth's child would inherit the land he redeems. He's not feeling very brotherly.

SHARON: There's actually ambiguity about who would get Ruth. Some translations have Boaz say to the redeemer, "On the day you acquire the property, *I* acquire Ruth." This implies that Boaz and Ruth already made it in the maize. Either way, Ruth's child would still inherit the bought land in the end. I must say I prefer the reading that says they wait for the marriage agreement. There's promise of fulfillment in everything.

MARION: All the same, a kinsman refuses to "raise up seed," as they say, for his dead brother. But Ruth raises up seed for her mother-in-law! When Ruth's child is born it's placed in Naomi's arms. The women say, "A son is born to Naomi!" There are rewards all around. Ruth gets rest and a baby, marriage to a kind man, and an honorable place in that society. A nice enough picture. But gloomy, too, since that's all there is to the woman's covenant. Women aren't directed to go anywhere, to do anything. Only their minds and emotions move; physically they're planted.

SHARON: But not in this case, since Naomi and Ruth walk out into life, and between them they get a baby! A progenitor of David! And a few generations later King David, descended from that threshing-floor encounter, will run a short flight upstairs to a house roof, where he gazes lustfully at naked Bathsheba, the wife of another man. When we compare the fate of those babies, we see that Ruth's, the child of honorable intentions all around, thrives in his grandmother's arms and in history. Bathsheba's and David's child, born of a love that betrays Bathsheba's husband—David's faithful follower, Uriah—is stricken and dies. We're in a world ruled by God's moral order. Wonderful! But we don't have more mother-daughter stories. Maybe because powerful women in groups have worried the rabbis. They were fearful of those old goddess religions from which some of these Bible stories may have emerged, carefully Hebraized. If once, for example, you start thinking of Naomi and Ruth as Demeter and Persephone, with their terrific power over the land, the seasons, the ability of earth to renew itself, you see how the whole story dances around the edges of fertility goddess ideas. One false move and there goes monotheism! But why can't we have a system of laws, of moral order, that doesn't suppress the female?

CHORUS: —You see? Paganism again!

—Bring in powerful women and everyone starts to worry . . .

—Quick! they say. Close the gates! Idolatry! The goddesses are coming!

MARION: There are plenty of other stories echoed here! Ruth sets out like Abraham. Both leave the place where they were born and go to a strange land. And both Ruth and Abraham are progenitors of a line of covenant inheritors! But only the male descendants of Abraham or Ruth hold the keys to the citadel! I really wish I could stop going on about that! But I can't. As far as I'm concerned, that's the top of the agenda.

SHARON: But once you've said it, it's understood! If you *only* say that, you've fallen into a trap of your own making. Then there's no way to reclaim our own texts. Their glory is withheld from us!

MARION: I give up, if you want glory at any price!

SHARON: I don't! I know we've all been kept outside and starved for centuries. When they finally let us into the palace, we don't want to just look at crumbs under the table. I want to see the whole banquet, even if I'm not allowed one taste!

MARION: I hate to say it, but that's slave mentality, taking pride in all the possessions of the big house, even though . . .

SHARON: I understand the need to hit out at these things, because we've been hit by them often enough. But we can't just lash out always, can we? Just mock and satirize and be negative and angry? Then we ourselves will have lost the gifts these stories have brought to human life!

MARION: What gifts, Sharon? I don't see how you let yourself romanticize in this way.

SHARON: What *gifts?* Why—whatever we've been saying! Even if everything is formula, even if stories are instilling moral behavior like Victorian children's tales, simplistic or narrow, these are what touch our hearts, move us, teach us values. Oh, don't make me drag it all out so boringly! You know perfectly well . . .

MARION: I'll do without it.

SHARON: Will you? Can you? I don't think I can, or want to. I can't go through literature with an ax, smashing things because women are badly portrayed in them, like some Carry Nation in a saloon!

MARION (*half rising*): If you're going to say that critical thinking is only smash and destroy . . .

SHARON: No, of course I don't mean that . . .

CHORUS: —We seem to be getting further and further from the real story!

—I feel tears welling up whenever I read it or even think about it.

—That's nothing to be ashamed of.

—Why can't we talk about that?

MARION (*bursts out again suddenly*): But it's such a rotten age!

SHARON: You mean that biblical one?

MARION: No—ours!

SHARON (*stands*): Let's not give up on ours too quickly.

I think we should break for a few minutes, and then go back and look at what we've left out.

4. No Going Back but by Going Forward: Sharon and Evelyn

SHARON (*with sympathy*): Tell us what parts of the story make you cry, Evelyn.

EVELYN: It may not be what you think. Not when Ruth says to Naomi, Anywhere you go, I go, too. It's not that obvious. It's when Boaz says to Ruth, "I have been told of all that you did for your mother-in-law after the death of your husband." He's heard of her kindness to the dead and to Naomi. My God, I took care of my father when he was dying for two whole years, and my sisters say to me, "What did you ever do for Daddy?" I can't bear to defend myself, or remind them of what I did. But not to be understood, not to be known—that's when I feel a true absence of God! Boaz understands, remembers, values what should be valued. Boaz sees and hears, he knows. He rewards goodness, he's like God, or like what we *want* God to be.

SHARON: Yes, all right, but why, for goodness' sake, take what's clearly for once a woman's story and make it into a man's story? Boaz like God! Why not Naomi like God?

EVELYN: No, she's too poor, too stripped, she has no largesse to bestow. She's exactly not God. She's quintessentially human, using brains, shrewdness, energy, to attract God's attention—or get away from God's attention, may be more like it. All right, no one is like God, but everyone important comes close to godlike actions. Everybody does the right thing—for once! And then again, it's when Ruth tells Boaz, "Now spread your wing over your maid-servant, for you are a redeemer." Don't ask me why. Unless it's because Boaz also says to Ruth, "May you have a full recompense from the Lord, the God of Israel, under whose wings you have sought refuge!" Boaz makes the connection, with language bridging to Ruth's. He may not be like God, but he knows how like God a man should be. And that, for me, comes close enough to tears.

SHARON (*sighs*): A perfect husband?

EVELYN: Don't try to joke it away!

SHARON: And don't think tears don't well up for me, too. For me it's that question Naomi asks Ruth when she comes back from her night with Boaz. Though I didn't realize it until I heard myself telling it.

EVELYN: When Ruth eats in the field, she takes from her own meal to bring to Naomi. I can't help thinking of Lear, who begs his daughters, "Oh, reason not the need," when they ask why he needs so much for his upkeep. Ruth is always adding more than good measure. So much of the text is about food, subsistence, gleaning, grain. Enough and more than enough, which is I guess what generosity is about. Here there's more generosity, more love, more courtesy than any ordinary family of relatives can give. What the story's telling me is that here at last is enough to feed the soul. Made-up stories invent characters that fill the need reality can't fill. Characters treating one another with tenderness, courtesy, and care. I never realized until this minute that Ruth and Boaz are like my favorite people in all of English literature—Elizabeth Bennett and Mr. Darcy! Though without any of their defensive wit. The expectations of a person of purity and virtue are met with purity and virtue. Ah, God, when's the last time that happened on earth? And why did it stop?

SHARON: Maybe it never started. Maybe it happens only in fantasy, invention, art. Or in religion. Be careful, Evelyn.

EVELYN: Two seconds in the Garden of Eden, maybe. Then it stopped.

SHARON: And that was invention, too. Maybe it's invention we have to be careful not to stop!

EVELYN (*becoming tearful*): Don't be clever with me. I want to go back to ideas of loyalty, devotion, honorableness! Mothers and daughters who care for one another, relatives who take responsibility for each other. I want to talk about continuity in a world where everything is getting lost.

SHARON: Poor Evelyn! You're the youngest of us, it's worst for you.

EVELYN: We've lost all that. We're barely willing to recognize what we're reading—plain, unironic goodness and virtue. *(Laughs shakily.)* "Honk if you love your mother!" I actually saw that on a bumper sticker on the parkway! I wanted to see who was driving, but I couldn't. I didn't hear anybody honk, and I didn't honk, either!

SHARON: You think it's entirely our fault we don't identify with *Ruth?* I'm not so sure! *Ruth* may be timeless, but it's not for our times. Nothing and no one is satirized. You know that's intolerable to modern temperament.

EVELYN: What in God's name is there to satirize here?

SHARON: Everything can be satirized if you look a certain way.

EVELYN: I challenge you on that. I don't see how you can.

SHARON: It takes a little effort, but not too much. Here. We all suspect that Naomi really hates her daughters-in-law, don't we? Obviously, she blames them for the deaths of her sons. The story, if I remember, doesn't say how the sons died, but if the women had been better wives, would this have happened? And we know already about Naomi sending Ruth out to seek fortune for both of them. We know a mother wouldn't have sent her own child, never! Naomi doesn't mind risking Ruth. She's got no clear plan. She just lets her daughter-in-law out like a monkey on a string as lure, as bait, to see who she can trap. And what's beautiful about this old man, this Boaz, who's perfectly willing to use up a young woman's life?

EVELYN (*crying out*): Oh, stop it, stop! Stop! Are we so willing to give up the beauty of our own texts because we're women? On Shavuot, we celebrate the giving of the Torah!

SHARON: To men, I'm awfully tempted to say! Should we ignore the taking away of it from women?

EVELYN: But in revolt against that theft, must we empty ourselves of our own stories?

SHARON: The truth is, men are as bereft as we are. Men or women—we live in the same sour, skeptical age. We've lost our absolutes.

EVELYN: Worse than lost. We badmouth them, act as if to believe in them robs us of our right to lay claim to intellect.

CHORUS: —Our age has lost it all.

—The beauty.

—The purity.

—The innocence.

EVELYN: The love!

SHARON: The willingness even to believe in it!

CHORUS: —Our lawyers love to find loopholes.

—Our literary critics love irony and satire.

—We're used to sniffing out ulterior motives.

—To hearing about betrayals.

—We love to think about unconscious motives.

EVELYN: Our writers punish characters in their stories with their own worst suspicions. They find decay everywhere, but never explain their own thriving!

SHARON: We put on the mantles of prophets and castigate, castigate, but then the mantles fall from our shoulders because we know no standards to uphold.

CHORUS: —If we knew them we wouldn't believe in them.

—We'd think they were too soft, too beautiful.

—Too pure, too unlikely.

—Too innocent, too soppy and cloying.

—Too sentimental, going on about "love."

—We'd miss the satire.

—We'd miss hearing about betrayals.

—We'd want to think about everybody's unconscious motives.

—We'd want to show how ridiculous and awful everybody is, compared to something or other, but we can't remember what.

—We scoff at stories of unselfish love.

—But even while we scoff we still feel the tears come.

—That is our hope.

EVELYN: That is our salvation.

SHARON: No, not salvation, only a sign that we may still thaw.

EVELYN: Yes, that's the necessary, the only sign.

CHORUS: (*The women stand and speak in unison, heads bowed, fists striking their hearts, as in the chorused* Al Het *recitations on Yom Kippur.*):

—for the sin of suspecting self-interest in all virtue,

—for the sin of skepticism toward love,

—for the sin of knowing Freud,

—for the sin of not knowing Freud,

—for the sin of breaking with the past,

—for the sin of not breaking with the past,

—for the sin of subservience to a man,

—for the sin of not living up to being a woman,

—for the sin of thinking children are our only fulfillment,

—for the sin of thinking children are not even necessary to our fulfillment,

—for the sin of thinking only of self-fulfillment,

—for the sin of not living for the good of community,

—for the sin of living only for others and forgetting self,

—for the sin of letting relatives dominate one's life,

—for the sin of forgetting family,

—for the sin of abandoning love of God and substituting romantic, erotic love,

—for the sin of not embracing romantic, erotic love and longing only for godlike love. . . .

(*The women now speak singly, each starting the moment the previous one stops.*)

SHARON: Oh hear us, God whose masculine form we can't believe in . . .

MARION: Oh answer us, God whose physical form we could not believe in, even if presented to us as female . . .

BECKY: Oh guide us and make us whole, fractured God who requires human deeds to fuse the scattered attributes at last . . .

LAURA: Judgment always joined with mercy, with beauty, with knowledge, with wisdom, with law, with goodness . . .

MARION: Oh stay with us, unlikely God, as Ruth stayed with Naomi . . .

BECKY: Help us to remember the secret syllables that revive our encounter on the threshing floor.

EVELYN: Oh, stay with us, unlikely God, stripped of power and impoverished, as Ruth stayed with Naomi, who was stripped of power and impoverished . . .

LAURA: Though it hardly seems worth Your while, or Ruth's while, or Naomi's while . . .

BECKY: Yet who knows whether we might, after irretrievable losses, encounter once more . . .

SHARON: Oh, stay with us, unlikely God, as Ruth stayed with Naomi, though it hardly seemed worth her while, until she awakened in Naomi's withered life new energy for encounter, which in the end brought both to redemption. *(Raises her head.)* I guess we stop now.

(*One by one, the women embrace Sharon and leave.*)

SHARON: (circles the room collecting cups and glasses, then looks up, meditative): The *Book of Ruth* closes with celebration of a boy's birth, a living bead on the covenantal string that's meant to reach us from our ancient past. Yet it's Naomi's question that stays with me. "How is it with you, my daughter?" "Who *are* you, my daughter?"

What is my answer?

(*Sharon exits, bearing away her burden of assorted vessels and food.*)